GERMAN FOR SINGERS

A Textbook of Diction and Phonetics

THIRD EDITION

GERMAN FOR SINGERS

A Textbook of Diction and Phonetics

THIRD EDITION

William Odom
Professor of German
University of Southern Mississippi

Prof. Mag.art Benno Schollum
Universität für Musik und darstellende Kunst Wien

Christina Balsam Curren
Associate Professor of German and German Lyric Diction
Eastman School of Music

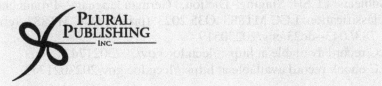

PLURAL
PUBLISHING
INC.

9177 Aero Drive, Suite B
San Diego, CA 92123

email: information@pluralpublishing.com
website: https://www.pluralpublishing.com

Copyright © 2025 by Plural Publishing, Inc.

Typeset in 11.5/14 LaserIPA by Flanagan's Publishing Services, Inc.
Printed in the United States of America by Integrated Books International

The LaserIPA in Unicode font used to print this work is available from Linguist's Software, Inc.,
PO Box 580, Edmonds, WA 98020-0580 USA tel (425) 775-1130 www.linguistsoftware.com

For permission to use material from this text, contact us by
Telephone: (866) 758–7251
Fax: (888) 758–7255
email: permissions@pluralpublishing.com

*Every attempt has been made to contact the copyright holders for material originally printed in another
source. If any have been inadvertently overlooked, the publisher will gladly make the necessary
arrangements at the first opportunity.*

Library of Congress Cataloging–in–Publication Data:
Names: Odom, William, 1939- author. | Schollum, Benno, author. | Curren,
  Christina Balsam, author.
Title: German for singers : a textbook of diction and phonetics / William
  Odom, Benno Schollum, Christina Balsam Curren.
Description: Third edition. | San Diego, CA : Plural Publishing, 2023.
Identifiers: LCCN 2023021742 (print) | LCCN 2023021743 (ebook) | ISBN
  9781635504248 (paperback) | ISBN 9781635504194 (ebook)
Subjects: LCSH: Singing--Diction. | German language--Pronunciation.
Classification: LCC MT883 .O35 2023 (print) | LCC MT883 (ebook) | DDC
  783/.043--dc23/eng/20230519
LC record available at https://lccn.loc.gov/2023021742
LC ebook record available at https://lccn.loc.gov/2023021743

Contents

PART I. Phonetics

PART II.
The Sounds of German

Preface to the Third Edition

The two main objectives of *German for Singers* put forth in the preface to the first edition continue to be: "(1) to give the singer a systematic approach to pronouncing any German word; and (2) to provide the singer with a phonetic shorthand for making notations above trouble spots in a score."

And as we found in the preface to the second edition, "even though *German for Singers* has been an effective tool for thousands of singers, we nevertheless felt that the book needed some changes, clarifications, and improvements in order to produce a more thorough familiarity with the subtleties of German diction." With this third edition of *German for Singers,* we hope to further improve and clarify our treatment of German diction and help build confidence in singers as they approach the extensive body of vocal literature in the German language.

INTERNATIONAL PHONETIC ALPHABET

As the use of the IPA has continued to proliferate, it has become challenging to maintain an overview of the different symbols in use. The long-time standard reference for stage and media professionals, *Deutsche Aussprache*, by Theodor Siebs, is now out of print, but still readily accessible at various sources, including e-book and print-on-demand options by the publisher. *Das Aussprachewörterbuch,* Volume 6 in the Duden German language series, is a reliable resource that, although oriented toward colloquial pronunciation, regularly reflects Siebs in most of its transcriptions and explanations.

In the third edition, we have adopted symbols now widely in use and have added, in footnotes as well as in the body of the text, variations in transcriptions as well as explanations of the use of various symbols, frequently citing Siebs in our comments. To underscore the challenge of making transcriptions, consider that the diphthong *au,* as in *Haus,* is transcribed in several standard sources variously as: [ɑo, ao, aɣ, aꭒ, au, aɔ, aʊ, aːo, aːu, aːʊ, a͜o,].

For the offglide in diphthongs we, like several sources, have elected to use the subscript arch, as in *Haus* [haọs], *Wein* [vaẹn].

We support the practice by citing Siebs, who states that it reflects the relationship of the dominant vowel to the non-syllabic vowel, although he elects not to indicate it in the transcriptions in *Deutsche Aussprache*.

Like most sources now, we indicate the syllable –*er* in *Vater* ['faːtɐ] with [ɐ], ['faːtɐ]; and, like Duden, we indicate vocalic *r* with [ɐ̯], as in *mir* [miːɐ̯] because it is in essence a diphthongal offglide, while holding open the artistic option to use a trill, depending on expressive intention.

RULES OF THUMB

Early in our discussion of German sounds, we have added a table of succinct rules of thumb regarding vowel length, stress, voicing, and pronunciation of *r*. Since these issues confront learners from the outset, we hope that condensing key concepts to a concise form will aid them in retaining and implementing the concepts as they progress through more challenging material.

STRESS

In Chapter 7, we attempt to address the issue of stress more thoroughly, dividing the prefixes into stressed, unstressed, or variable and including a discussion of secondary stress as well as a description of stress in words borrowed from other languages.

EXCEPTIONS

Included in every section on German pronunciation is a list of exceptions to the rules, with their translations. Quite a few of these occur regularly in vocal literature, and the serious student is urged to memorize as many as possible.

ANSWER KEYS

For the third edition, we have added a student section with answers to many exercises and a teacher section that contains answers to all exercises, as well as many other useful supplements. These sections can be accessed on the companion website.

TRANSLATIONS

With the addition of translations for the excerpts and song texts, we hope to extend our pragmatic treatment of the German language in singing to the meaning of the texts. Poetic translations and singable translations are available in various sources; with our translations, we want to help singers see the relationship of the German words to the English words, so that as they pronounce them they may see, as nearly as possible, what each word means. If at all possible, we have attempted to keep the English words on the same line as the German words and, when possible, to have an English word for each German word. We have used parentheses to add a word necessary for the English or to clarify a German word that cannot be comfortably rendered in the English. This is, of necessity, not a precise process, and may sometimes lead to somewhat stiff or prosaic phrasing, but we hope that having a good understanding of what each word means will enable singers to bring more confident expression to their performance.

RECORDINGS

We include audio recordings of most of the exercises and many of the excerpts in each chapter, which are spoken and sung by Benno Schollum. The items on the recordings are indicated in the text with the symbol shown here. These recordings can be accessed on the companion website.

We hope that, as a textbook and a reference, *German for Singers* will continue to provide beginning singers and more experienced singers alike with the tools they need to acquire a solid command of German diction and phonetics.

Recordings

Alphabetical Index

C = single consonant; CC = two or more consonants

Spelling		Pronunciation	Position	Examples	Page
a		[aː]	1. before C	sagen ['zaːgən] "to say"	131
			2. before *h*	ahnen ['aːnən] "to sense"	131
			3. doubled	Saal [zaːl] "hall"	131
			4. before CC in some words	nach [naːx] "toward"	132
				zart [tsaːɐt] "gentle"	132
		[a]	1. before CC	Mann [man] "man"	133
			2. before C in a few words	an [an] "to, at"	133
				das [das] "the"	133
	ai	[aɛ̯]	all positions	Mai [maɛ̯] "May"	164
	au	[aɔ̯]	all positions	Haus [haɔ̯s] "house"	163
	ay	[aɛ̯]	all positions	Bayer ['baɛ̯ɐ] "Bavarian"	164
ä[1]		[ɛː]	1. before C	spät [ʃpɛːt] "late"	138
			2. before *h*	Mähne ['mɛːnə] "mane"	138
			3. before CC in a few words	zärtlich ['tsɛːɐtlɪç] "gentle"	138
		[ɛ]	before CC	Händel ['hɛndəl]	139
	äu	[ɔɐ̯]	all positions	Häuser ['hɔɐ̯zɐ] "houses"	168
b		[b]	1. before vowel, *l* or *r* in one element	Eber ['eːbɐ] "boar"	114
				geblickt [gə'blɪkt] "glimpsed"	114
			2. before *l*, *n*, or *r* in derivatives or inflected forms	ebne ['eːbnə] "level" (<eben)	114
		[p]	1. final	Grab [ɡʀaːp] "grave"	114
			2. preconsonantal	liebst [liːpst] "(you) love"	114

[1]The vowel ä is sometimes spelled *ae;* the pronunciation remains the same.

Spelling	Pronunciation	Position	Examples	Page
		3. final in element	Halbinsel ['halpˌɪnzəl] "peninsula"	114
			abreisen ['apˌɾaɐzən] "depart"	114
bb	[b]	in one element	Ebbe ['ɛbə] "ebb"	114
	[pb]	in two elements	abbauen ['apˌbaɒən] "dismantle"	114
c	[ts]	before a front vowel	Cicero ['tsiːtsero]	207
	[k]	before a back vowel	Cafe [kaˈfeː] "cafe"	207
ch	[x]	after a back vowel	Bach [bax]	41
	[ç]	after a front vowel or a consonant	ich [ɪç] "I"	41
			Mädchen ['mɛːtçən] "girl"	41
	[k]	in some words of Greek origin	Orchester [ɔrˈkɛstɐ] "orchestra"	208
chs	[ks]	in one element	sechs [zɛks] "six"	214
	varied	in two elements	see Chapter 15	214
ck	[k]	all positions	nicken ['nɪkən] "nod"	201
d	[d]	1. before vowel or *r* in one element	Ader ['aːdɐ] "artery"	118
			bedrohen [bəˈdɾoːən] "threaten"	118
		2. before l, n, or r in derivatives or inflected forms	edler ['eːdlɐ] "noble" (<edel)	118
	[t]	1. final	Freund [frɔɵnt] "friend"	118
		2. preconsonantal	widmen ['vɪtmən] "dedicate"	118
		3. final in element	fremdartig ['frɛmtˌaːɐtɪç] "strange"	118
dd	[d]	in one element	Widder ['vɪdɐ] "ram"	119

Spelling		Pronunciation	Position	Examples	Page
		[td]	in two elements	Raddampfer [ˈraːtˌdampfɐ] "paddle wheeler"	119
	dt	[t]	in one element	Städte [ˈʃtɛːtə] "cities"	119
		[tt]	in two elements	Handtuch [ˈhantˌtuːx] "towel"	119
e		[eː]	1. before C	beten [ˈbeːtən] "pray"	65
			2. before *h*	geht [geːt] "goes"	65
			3. doubled	Beet [beːt] "(flower)bed"	65
			4. before CC in some words	Erde [ˈeːɐdə] "earth"	65
				stets [ʃteːts] "always"	66
		[ɛ]	1. before CC	Bett [bɛt] "bed"	66
			2. before C in a few words	des [dɛs] "of the"	66
				weg [vɛk] "away"	66
			3. in the prefixes *er-, her-, ver-, zer-*	erfahren [ɛɐˈfaːrən] "experience"	67
		[ə]	1. final unstressed	Liebe [ˈliːbə] "love"	68
			2. medial unstressed	liebevoll [ˈliːbəfɔl] "loving"	68
			3. unstressed prefixes and endings	"beginnen [bəˈgɪnən] "begin"	68
				meines [ˈmaɛnəs] "of my"	68
	ei	[aɛ]	in one element	mein [maɛn] "my"	164
	eu	[ɔø]	in one element	Leute [ˈlɔøtə] "people"	168
	ey	[aɛ]	in all positions	Meyer [ˈmaɛɐ] a surname	164
f		[f]	in all positions	fein [faɛn] "fine"	223
	ff	[f]	in one element	treffen [ˈtrɛfən] "meet"	223
		[ff]	in two elements	auffahren [ˈaɔfˌfaːrən] "rise"	223
g		[g]	1. before vowel, *l*, or *r* in one element	Geld [gɛlt] "money"	124
				Glück [glʏk] "happiness"	124

Spelling	Pronunciation	Position	Examples	Page
		2. before *l*, *n*, or *r* in derivatives or inflected forms	eigner ['aɛgnɐ] "own" (<eigen)	124
	[k]	1. final	lag [laːk] "was lying"	124
		2. preconsonantal	klagt [klaːkt] "laments"	124
		3. final in element	bergab [ˌbɛɾkˈlap] "downhill"	124
		4. in *-ig* before *-lich*	königlich ['køːnɪklɪç] "royal"	125
	[ç]	in *-ig* when final or preconsonantal	heilig ['haɛlɪç] "holy"	125
			heiligt ['haɛlɪçt] "consecrates"	125
	[ʒ]	in some words of French origin	Genie [ʒeˈniː]	124
gg	[g]	in one element	Flagge ['flagə] "flag"	125
	[kg]	in two elements	weggehen ['vɛkˌgeːən] "go away"	126
gn	[gn]	in one element	Gnade ['gnaːdə] "mercy"	125
h	[h]	initially in a word or element	Hand [hant] "hand"	185
			woher [voˈheːɐ] "whence"	185
	silent	elsewhere after a vowel	Floh [floː] "flea"	185
i	[iː]	1. before C	mir [miːɐ] "me"	53
		2. before *h*	ihn [iːn] "him"	53
	[ɪ]	1. before CC	bist [bɪst] "(you) are"	53
		2. in the suffixes *-in*, *-nis*, *-ig*	Freundin ['frɔøndɪn] "(girl) friend"	54
			Kenntnis ['kɛntnɪs] "knowledge"	54
			giftig ['gɪftɪç] "poisonous"	54
		3. in *-ik* if unstressed	Lyrik ['lyːɾɪk] "lyrics"	54
		4. in some short words before C	mit [mɪt] "with"	54
			in [ɪn] "in"	54

Spelling		Pronunciation	Position	Examples	Page
	ie	[iː]	all positions except final in some words	die [diː] "the"	142
				Melodie [meloˈdiː]	142
		[i̯ə]	final in some words	Lilie [ˈliːli̯ə] "lily"	143
j		[j]	in most words	ja [jaː] "yes"	187
				Major [maˈjoːɐ̯]	187
		[ʒ]	in some words of French origin	Journal [ʒʊrˈnaːl]	187
k		[k]	in all positions	kaum [kaͻm] "hardly"	201
	kk	[k]	in one element	Akkord [aˈkͻrt] "chord"	201
	kn	[kn]	in all positions	Knabe [ˈknaːbə] "lad"	201
l		[l] "light l"	in all positions	hell [hɛl] "bright"	173
	ll	[l] "light l"	in one element	fülle [ˈfʏlə] "fill"	174
		[l͜l] "light l"	in two elements	fühllos [ˈfyːl͜loːs] "unfeeling"	174
m		[m]	in all positions	mein [maͧn] "my"	225
	mm	[m]	in one element	Flamme [ˈflamə] "flame"	225
		[m͜m]	in two elements	ummalen [ˈʊm͜maːlən] "repaint"	225
n		[n]	in all positions	nein [naͧn] "no"	226
	ng	[ŋ]	in one element	Finger [ˈfɪŋɐ] "finger"	227
		[ng]	in two elements	hingehen [ˈhɪnˌgeːən] "go there"	227
	nk	[ŋk]	in one element	dunkel [ˈdʊŋkəl] "dark"	227
		[nk]	in two elements	ankommen [ˈanˌkͻmən] "arrive"	227
	nn	[n]	in one element	Tanne [ˈtanə] "fir tree"	226
		[n͜n]	in two elements	annehmen [ˈanˌneːmən] "accept"	226

Spelling		Pronunciation	Position	Examples	Page
o		[oː]	1. before C	schon [ʃoːn] "already"	78
				groß [gʁoːs] "great"	79
			2. before *h*	ohne ['oːnə] "without"	78
			3. doubled	Boot [boːt] "boat"	78
			4. before CC in some words	e.g. hoch [hoːx] "high"	78
				Trost [tʁoːst] "solace"	79
		[ɔ]	1. before CC	doch [dɔx] "but"	79
			2. before C in a few words	ob [ɔp] "whether"	80
				von [fɔn] "of"	80
ö[2]		[øː]	1. before *h*	fröhlich ['fʁøːlɪç] "merry"	72
			2. before C	schön [ʃøːn] "lovely"	72
				größer ['gʁøːsɐ] "greater"	72
			3. before CC in some words	trösten ['tʁøːstən] "console"	72
		[œ]	before CC	möchte ['mœçtə] "would like"	73
p		[p]	in all positions	Pein [paɛn] "pain"	174
	pf	[pf]	in all positions	Pfad [pfaːt] "path"	195
	ph	[f]	in all positions	Phantasie [fanta'ziː] "fantasy"	195
	pp	[p]	in one element	Lippe ['lɪpə] "lip"	194
	ps	[ps]	in all positions	Psalm [psalm] "psalm"	195
qu		[kv]	in all positions	Qualität [kvali'tɛːt] "quality"	203
r		[ɐ̯]	1. final	mir [miːɐ̯] "me"	37
				Bier [biːɐ̯] "beer"	37
			2. preconsonantal after long vowel	werden ['veːɐ̯dən] "become"	180

---

[2]The vowel *ö* is sometimes spelled *oe*; the pronunciation remains the same.

Spelling		Pronunciation	Position	Examples	Page
			3. final in element	vergessen [fɛɐ̯'gɛsən] "forget"	179
		[ɐ]	in the suffix *-er*	bitter ['bɪtɐ] "bitter"	38
		[ɾ]	1. prevocalic	raten ['raːtən] "advise"	36
				fahren ['faːɾən] "drive"	36
				fragen ['fraːgən] "ask"	36
			2. preconsonantal after short vowel	warten ['vaɾtən] "wait"	180
	rr	[ɾ]	in one element	sperren ['ʃpɛɾən] "lock"	180
				Herr [hɛɾ] "Lord, gentleman"	180
		[ɐɾ]	in two elements, as a rule	Vorrede ['foːɐ̯ˌreːdə] "introduction"	180
s		[z]	1. before a vowel	singen ['zɪŋən] "sing"	147
			2. before *l*, *n*, or *r* in derivatives or inflected forms	unsre ['ʊnzɾə] "our" (<unser)	147
		[s]	1. final	als [als] "when"	147
				Betrugs [bə'truːks] "of deceit"	147
			2. before a consonant	Dresden ['dɾeːsdən]	147
			3. final in element	Lesart ['leːsˌaːɐ̯t] "version"	147
			4. before a vowel in some words	e.g. Erbse ['ɛɾpsə] "pea"	147
	sch	[ʃ]	in one element	Schule [ʃuːlə] "school"	158
		[sç]	in two elements	Röschen ['røːsçən] "little rose"	158
	sp	[ʃp]	initial in element	spielen [ʃpiːlən] "play"	155
				Glockenspiel ['glɔkənʃpiːl]	155
		[sp]	1. medial or final in one element	Wespe [vɛspə] "wasp"	155

Spelling	Pronunciation	Position	Examples	Page
		2. in two elements	Liebespaar ['li:bəsˌpaːɐ̯] "couple"	155
			ausprägen ['aʊsˌprɛːgən] "stamp"	155
ss	[s]	in one element	müssen ['mʏsən] "must"	149
	varied	in two elements	see Chapter 10	149
st	[ʃt]	initial in element	stellen ['ʃtɛlən] "place"	155
			verstellen [vɛɐ̯'ʃtɛlən] "disguise"	155
	[st]	1. medial or final in one element	Laster ['lastɐ] "vice"	155
			ist [ɪst] "is"	155
		2. superlative -st	schnellste ['ʃnɛlstə] "fastest"	155
		3. in two elements	austragen ['aʊsˌtraːgən] "carry out"	155
ß	[s]	in all positions	Gruß ['gruːs] "greeting"	148
			Grüße ['gryːsə] "greetings"	148
t	[t]	in all positions	Tal [taːl] "valley"	199
th	[t]	in one element	Theater [te'aːtɐ] "theater"	199
	[th]	in two elements	Rathaus ['raːtˌhaʊs] "town hall"	199
ti	[tsi̯]	in the syllable -tion	Nation [na'tsi̯oːn] "nation"	200
tsch	[tʃ]	in one element	Deutsch [dɔʏtʃ] "German"	199
tt	[t]	in one element	Fittich ['fɪtɪç] "wing"	199
	[tt]	in two elements	Bettag ['beːtˌtaːk] "day of prayer"	199
tz	[ts]	in one element	setzen ['zɛtsən] "set"	189
	[tts]	in two elements	entzücken [ɛntˌtsʏkən] "delight"	189

Spelling		Pronunciation	Position	Examples	Page
u		[uː]	1. before C	Mut [muːt] "courage"	85
				Gruß [gɾuːs] "greeting"	86
			2. before *h*	Ruhe ['ɾuːə] "rest"	85
			3. before CC in some words	Buch [buːx] "book"	86
		[ʊ]	1. before CC	Kunst [kʊnst] "art"	86
			2. before C in some words	um [ʊm] "around"	87
				zum [tsʊm] "to the"	87
ü[3]			1. before C	für [fyːɐ̯] "for"	58
				grüßen ['gɾyːsən] "greet"	59
			2. before *h*	fühle ['fyːlə] "feel"	58
			3. before CC in some words	Bücher ['byːçɐ̯] "books"	59
				düster ['dyːstɐ̯] "somber"	59
		[ʏ]	before CC	fünf [fʏnf] "five"	60
				müssen ['mʏsən] "must"	60
v		[f]	in words of Germanic origin	viel [fiːl] "much"	222
		[v]	in most words of foreign origin	Vase ['vaːzə] "vase"	222
w		[v]	in all positions	Wein [va̯ẹn] "wine"	217
x		[ks]	in all positions	Hexe ['hɛksə] "witch"	203
y		[yː]	before C	Lyrik ['lyːɾɪk] "lyrics"	58
		[ʏ]	before CC	idyllisch [iˈdʏlɪʃ] "idyllic"	60
z		[ts]	in all positions	Zeit [tsa̯ẹt] "time"	189
				Kreuz [kɾɔø̯ts] "cross"	189
	zz	[ts]	in words of Italian origin	Skizze ['skɪtsə] "sketch"	189

C = Single consonant; CC = two or more consonants.

---

[3]The vowel *ü* is sometimes spelled *ue*; the pronunciation remains the same.

Reviewers

Plural Publishing and the authors would like to thank the following reviewers for taking the time to provide their valuable feedback during the manuscript development process.

About the Authors

William Odom is professor of German language and music diction at the University of Southern Mississippi. He has provided coaching for concerts, recitals, and opera productions, including at the New Orleans Opera. He has published a number of translations, including *Hörspiel*, a collection of radio dramas, and *JAZZ: A Photo History* by Joachim-Ernst Berendt. He authored the first edition of *German for Singers*, which appeared in 1981, and has continued to play a central role in the development of subsequent editions.

Benno Schollum, Austrian baritone, studied at the University of Music and the Performing Arts in Vienna, and has held a teaching post there for 40 years, as well as annual master classes since its inception at the Franz Schubert Institute in 1978. He has been a guest professor at the Sibelius Academy in Helsinki, at London's Royal Academy and Royal College of Music. He combines teaching with an active singing career with repertoire extending from the great oratorios to opera, operetta, musicals, lieder, chansons and Viennese music. He has performed around the globe with, among others, the Berlin Philharmonic, San Francisco Symphony, Royal Philharmonic Orchestra, and Vienna Symphony with conductors such as Yehudi Menuhin, Mstislav Rostropovich, Philippe Entremont, Adam Fischer, Zoltán Kocsis, Vladimir Fedoseyev and James Judd. He played the role of Kuno in the movie of Carl Maria von Weber's opera *Der Freischütz* and has recorded Schubert's *Winterreise,* Haydn's *Creation*, Händel's *Messiah*, Beethoven's 9th Symphony, Schubert Masses, Tchaikovsky's *Iolanta,* and most recently *Viennese Songs.*

Christina Balsam Curren spent 7 years as a repertory coach at the Niedersächsische Staatsoper in Hannover, Germany. This followed postgraduate studies in collaborative piano, opera coaching, lyric diction, and voice at the Hochschule für Musik und Darstellende Kunst "Mozarteum" (now Universität Mozarteum) in Salzburg, Austria, where she also taught in the opera school for 2 years. She has given classes and worked with singers, instrumentalists, and diverse choral and opera groups in many European countries and the United States. She has coached German diction and provided English translations for German choral and stage works for churches, the Eastman/Christ Church Schola Cantorum, the Chicago-based early music collective Schola Antiqua, Ohio Light Opera, Eastman Opera Theatre, and the Nazareth College Opera Workshop. Since 1989 she has taught at the Eastman School of Music, where she is a vocal coach and a professor of German and German lyric diction, assisting singers, collaborative pianists, and conductors in deepening their understanding of (and, hopefully, delight in) the nuances of German text and vocal music.

PART I

Phonetics

1

Introduction to Phonetics

THE IPA

Consider the words *ski, key, quay, me, meat, meet, siege, seize, people,* and *amoeba*. They all contain the vowel sound traditionally represented in dictionaries by the symbol *ē*.

Now consider the words *wage, wag, wad, wall, ago,* and *many*. Although the vowel *a* appears in each word, it represents a different sound in each; these sounds have been traditionally indicated as *ā, ă, ä, ô, ə,* and *ĕ*, respectively.

If we now include foreign languages in our discussion, it becomes clear that the sound *ē* has a number of yet different spellings and that the letter *a* has a number of yet different pronunciations. Although the number of sounds that human beings use in speaking is limited, it is apparent that the variety of spellings for these sounds can be bewildering. To facilitate the business of learning pronunciation, it would seem logical to have a system in which one symbol represents one sound. The International Phonetic Association, which was founded in 1886, had as one of its chief objectives to create just such a system. The result was the International Phonetic Alphabet, or IPA. Although not the only such alphabet, the IPA has become the most widely accepted one and is used in many of the standard references consulted by singers.

German for Singers offers the singer active practice in transcribing sounds into the IPA. Every singer needs a shorthand for jotting down pronunciations. As often as not, the singer will not copy a transcription directly from a reference book but will note down on

3

a score a pronunciation that is troublesome, or a correction given by a teacher or coach. In either event, it is convenient to have a ready command of the IPA in order to note down a pronunciation. Furthermore, if skill is achieved in writing the IPA, then it will be even easier for the singer to read transcriptions.

VARIATIONS IN SOUNDS

The exercises in the following chapters will generate lively discussions over which symbols to use in certain instances. Two factors must be taken into consideration in trying to resolve such questions.

First, one should consider the range of speech sounds as a continuum, much like the light spectrum. When we think of green, a variety of colors comes to mind. What we consider to be green is actually a somewhat arbitrarily chosen section of wavelengths that fades into yellow on one end and into blue on the other. Likewise, each IPA symbol represents not one sound, but a family of closely related sounds. Thus, the *t* sound is quite different in *top, stop, pot, rotten,* and *bottle* but will still be represented by [t] in the IPA.[1] Vowels also change their color depending on the nature of the consonants surrounding them. The *e* in *bed* does not have exactly the same sound as the *e* in *bet* or *bell*, but all may be represented by the IPA symbol [ɛ]. So, just as the word *green* can indicate a variety of shades, the symbols [t] or [ɛ] can indicate a range of sounds.

Second, the choice of a symbol for a certain sound is affected by individual pronunciation. Differences in accent will give rise to differences in pronunciation. But even within the same dialect group there can be differences in pronunciation.

In *German for Singers*, we will focus on standard pronunciation for both English and German.

---

[1]The IPA has developed diacritic marks to reflect such subtleties of difference.

Transcribing Sounds

THE SYMBOLS

Before we begin a discussion of transcription, a few notes on the conventions followed in transcribing are in order.

Sound Versus Letter

A *sound* is always represented by an IPA symbol in square brackets: [t]; a *letter* is printed in italics: *t*.

Stress

The main, or primary, stress in a word is indicated by a short vertical line above and to the left of the syllable, as in *intend* [ɪnˈtɛnd]. The secondary stress heard in some words is indicated with a short vertical line below and to the left of the syllable, as in *episode* [ˈɛpɪˌsoʊd].

Length

In the IPA, *length* refers to the amount of *time* it takes to pronounce a sound, not to the quality of the sound. Thus the vowel in *mad* is actually longer than the vowel in *mate,* although traditionally the sound of *a* in *mate* would be called "long *a*" and indicated as ā. In IPA transcription, length is indicated with a colon. The word *beat* might appear as [bit], and the word *bead,* which has a longer vowel sound, might appear in transcription as [biːd].

Vowel length will not be reflected in transcriptions of English words in this book. The use of the symbol for vowel length in German is discussed in Chapter 6.

Symbols

One of the great advantages of the IPA is that it is based on our alphabet. Many of the symbols for sounds are identical with the letters that typically represent the sounds. Thus, the sound of the letter *t* is represented by the symbol [t]. The student should note that the following consonant symbols are used to denote the sounds most commonly associated with these letters: [b, d, f, g, h, k, l, m, n, p, s, t, v, w, z].

Note on r: Although many sources transcribe the English r as [r], we will transcribe it as [ɹ].

Symbol Names

Although the International Phonetic Association has not officially approved a set of names, many symbols have commonly used names, and we will include those in parentheses when introducing the symbol.

One Sound:
One Symbol

When transcribing, do not be misled by spelling; always assign a symbol for each sound. Often, several letters are used to represent one sound, such as *ough* in *bought*, which is transcribed [bɔt]. Conversely, one letter may be used to represent two or more sounds, such as *x* in *fix*, which is transcribed [fɪks].

No punctuation, such as a capital or an apostrophe within a word, is reflected in IPA transcription. Thus *Pete's* is rendered as [pits].

VOWELS

Monophthongs

[i] (lower-case I)
[ɪ] (small capital I)

The symbol [i] represents the sound of *i* in *ski*. It represents this sound regardless of how it is spelled. Thus we see that the words listed at the beginning of this section—*ski, key, quay, me, meat, meet, siege, seize, people, amoeba*—would be transcribed [ski, ki, ki, mi, mit, mit, siʒ, siz, ˈpipəl, əˈmibə].

The symbol [ɪ] represents the sound of *i* in *skit*, which is transcribed as [skɪt].

Exercise 2.1   Transcribe the following words:

1. pit, peat, Pete
2. bit, bits, bead, beads
3. nick, Nick, nix, nicks, Nick's
4. deep, dip, dips, dipped
5. be, been, bean, beans
6. fill, fills, filled, field
7. kick, quick, squeak, squeaked
8. sieve, seize, peace, piece, please

[ɛ] (epsilon)
[æ] (ash *or* lower-case A-E ligature)

The symbol [ɛ] represents the vowel sound in *bed* [bɛd]. The symbol [æ] represents the vowel sound in *cat* [kæt].

Exercise 2.2   Transcribe the following words (Remember to transcribe *r* as [ɹ]):

1. bet, bat, fad, fads
2. bread, bred, breed, brad
3. guest, guessed, geese, passed
4. band, banned, fest, feast, fast
5. impact, infect, deeds, beds
6. Nat's, gnats, nest, knack

Exercise 2.3   Read the following transcriptions aloud, then write down the words they represent. Some may have more than one spelling.

1. [spɪn, splin, tæks, ɛk'spænd]
2. [sɪnd, sɛnt, bægz, tækt]
3. [dɪ'kænt, kiz, fɹiz, pæɹ]
4. [ɹɪ'list, dɪ'siv, 'ɹɛspɪt, ɹɪ'sɪnd]
5. [tɛkst, pik, 'æ‚spɛkt, 'klæsɪk, ɪm'pɹɛst]
6. [il, livz, fɪnz, ‚ækwɪ'ɛs]
7. [pɹɛst, kwɪn'tɛt, pɹɪs'tin, 'pæɹɪs]

[ɑ] (script A)
[ɔ] (open O)   The symbol [ɑ] represents the sound of *a* in *far* ['fɑɹ]. The symbol [ɔ] represents the vowel sound in *hall* [hɔl].

Exercise 2.4   Pronounce the following word pairs containing [ɑ] and [ɔ]:

1. fond - fawned
2. stock - stalk
3. bobble - bauble
4. body - bawdy
5. rot - wrought
6. knot - naught
7. popper - pauper

Exercise 2.5   Transcribe the following words:

1. all, awl, fall, pause, paws
2. cot, caught, Don, dawn
3. clawed, clod, naught, not
4. far, for, park, pork
5. wrought, rot, rat, gnawed, nod

[u] (lower-case U)
[ʊ] (horseshoe U)[1]   The symbol [u] represents the vowel sound in *boot* [but]. The symbol [ʊ] represents the vowel sound in *book* [bʊk].

Exercise 2.6   Transcribe the following words:

1. nook, put, full, fool, foot
2. moons, prove, lute, loot
3. look, Luke, cooed, could, cod
4. lose, loss, lost, loose
5. crew, crude, crook, crock
6. baboon, monsoon, festoon
7. spool, pull, would, wood

[ʌ] (turned V)
[ə] (schwa)   The symbol [ʌ] represents the vowel sound in *but* [bʌt]. The symbol [ə], called the *schwa*, is the sound of *a* in *approve* [əˈpɹuv]. Although the articulation of the two sounds is somewhat similar, [ə] appears *only* in unstressed syllables.

Exercise 2.7   Transcribe the following words:

1. bun, blood, fussed, flux
2. abet, collect, condemn, vista
3. above, conundrum, alumnus, compulsive
4. tough, son, woman, summons
5. buck, book, boot, putt, put, pool
6. symphony, sonata, accustomed

Exercise 2.8   Read the following transcriptions aloud, then write down the words they represent. Some may have more than one spelling.

1. [kəˈkafənɪ, ˈɑɹɪə, ˈlʌv, ˈsʌnz]
2. [kəˈdɛnzə, bəˈsun, ˈɑpəɹə, kwɑɹˈtɛt]
3. [ˌɹɛsɪtəˈtiv, kələɹəˈtuɹə, kənˈklusɪv]

---

[1]Also called "upside-down omega," this character is generally known as "upsilon," from the Latin small capital U.

4. [ˈɔɹɡən, ɹʌf, kɔf, ˈɔfəl]

5. [ˈɹɔkəs, ˈɹʌkəs, flu, luz]

6. [bɹʊk, wʊlvz, lus, bɹu, ˈkɹʊkɪd]

7. [lɔɹd, laɹd, hʊk, hɑk, hɔk]

8. [sɔt, sʊt, sɑt, sæt, sɛt, sɪt, sit, ˈsʌtlɪ]

9. [ɛɡˈzɔst, brˈkɔz, fɑks, ˌfʊlˈfɪl]

Sounds in Unstressed Syllables: [ɚ], [l̩]

Many sources use the symbol [ɚ], called a "right-hook schwa" to represent the final syllable *-er*, as in *sister* [ˈsɪstɚ]. The IPA describes this symbol as an "R-colored mid central vowel," indicating that the syllable consists of *r* and schwa blended together.

Some sources use the symbol [l̩] to represent the final sound in *people* [ˈpipl̩]. The IPA name for the diacritic under the *l* is "syllabicity mark," indicating that the syllable consists of *l* and the vowel blended together.

Depending on the source and on the context, these words can also be transcribed [ˈsɪstəɹ, ˈpipəl].

Exercise 2.9

Transcribe the following words:

1. rustle, fiddle, castle, lovable
2. cover, older, wander, banter

Diphthongs

The word *diphthong* comes from the Greek *di-*, "two," and *phthongos*, "sound." A diphthong begins with one vowel sound and ends with another. Although only two of the English diphthongs are regularly spelled with two vowels, there are at least five diphthongs in standard English: [ɔɪ, aʊ, aɪ, eɪ, oʊ]. In each of these diphthongs, the first vowel is the dominant sound, extending to over half the length of the diphthong and proceeding smoothly to the second vowel, also called the off-glide. It is important to note that a diphthong is a continuous sound occurring within one syllable.[2]

---

[2]A diacritic is sometimes used to indicate that the off-glide is to be treated as part of the diphthong, not as a separate syllable, e.g. [ɔɪ̯, aʊ̯]. (See Chapter 11 for German diphthongs.)

[ɔɪ, aʊ]   The diphthong [ɔɪ] is the vowel sound in *boy* [bɔɪ]. The diphthong [aʊ] is the vowel sound in *how* [haʊ]. Notice that we use the symbol [a] (lower-case A) instead of the symbol [ɑ] (script A) for the first part of this diphthong. The pronunciation of the sounds [a] and [ɑ] is discussed below.

Exercise 2.10   Transcribe the following words:

1. bough, boy, boil, bout

2. decoy, ploy, plough, noise

3. abound, anoint, hoist, Faust, clown

4. crowd, proud, about, royal

[aɪ, eɪ, oʊ]   There are three other sounds that must be considered phonetically as diphthongs even though they are frequently represented with only a single letter in spelling. These are [aɪ] as in *pile* [paɪl], [eɪ] as in *pale* [peɪl], and [oʊ] as in *pole* [poʊl]. Of course, these diphthongs have a variety of spellings, including some which apparently have a letter to represent the second element [ɪ] or [ʊ], such as *i* in *maid* [meɪd] or *w* in *low* [loʊ]. It is important to realize that there is no distinction in pronunciation between the vowel sound in *maid* and the vowel sound in *made;* both are transcribed with the diphthong [eɪ].

Exercise 2.11   Transcribe the following words:

1. ways, weighs, wades, waits, straight

2. load, lode, lowed, dough, mould

3. write, right, slight, sleight, slate

4. height, weight, receive, weird

5. stole, stale, stile, style, steel, still, stool

6. great, gray, mind, guide, aisle

7. sew, know, ago, aglow, blows

Exercise 2.12   Read the following transcriptions aloud, then write the words they represent. Some may have more than one spelling.

1. [ˈlɔɪəl, əˈbaʊt, sleɪ, veɪn, ɹoʊd]

2. [aɪl, laɪ, ɹɪˈfɹeɪn, ɹoʊm, ɹum, ɹʌm]

3. [taɪm, floʊz, loʊn, ˈkwaɪət, oʊ, maʊs]

4. [faɪl, foʊl, feɪl, fɔɪl, fil, fɪl, fɔl, fɛl, ful, ˈfɑlɪ, ˈfælo, fʌn

5. [ˈsoʊfə, aɪ, ɹeɪn, kəmˈpleɪn, soʊl]

English Diphthong vs. German Monophthong

With the sounds [eɪ] and [oʊ], it is very important to be aware of the second vowel of the diphthong: [ɪ], [ʊ]. The initial vowels of these diphthongs appear in English only in the diphthongs [eɪ] and [oʊ], but not separately as the vowels [e] and [o], except in some unstressed syllables. In German, as well as in other major European languages, the sounds [e] and [o] also appear as monophthongs in stressed syllables. Contrast the following:

English	*German*
bait [beɪt]	Beet [beːt]
boat [boʊt]	Boot [boːt]

To pronounce the German words using the English diphthong would result in a recognizable, and undesirable, accent. We treat these sounds in greater detail in Chapter 6.

[a] (lower-case A) vs. [ɑ] (script A)

In the diphthongs [aɪ] and [aʊ], a new symbol, [a], is introduced. Although the sound it represents does not occur in isolation in standard American English, it can be isolated for the sake of contrast by pronouncing the greeting *Hi!* [haɪ] or the verb *lie* [laɪ] and eliminating the second element of the diphthong: [ha], [la]. The sound thus obtained is different from the sound in the exclamation *Ha!* [hɑ] or the syllable *la* [lɑ] (as in *tra-la-la*), [ɑ] being more of a back vowel (sometimes referred to as "dark" *a*) and [a] being more of a front vowel (sometimes referred to as "bright" *a*). The sound [a] does exist in isolation in some accents, for example in the New England pronunciation of *Harvard* [ˈhaːvəd] or in the Deep South pronunciation of *dry wine* [dra wan]. (See Chapter 9 for a discussion of German *a*.)

CONSONANTS

The symbols for most consonant sounds are the same as the letters of the alphabet commonly used to represent the sounds. Some letters, however, have more than one pronunciation; and certain groups of letters represent a single sound. In both cases, some new symbols are required to represent the sounds.

[j] (lower-case J)

Although the sounds [j] and [w] are sometimes classified as *semi-vowels* or *glides*, they are treated in this text as consonants. The symbol [j] represents the sound of *y* in *yes* [jɛs] or the initial element of *u* in *use* [juz] or *fuse* [fjuz]. The sound has other spellings, which are illustrated in the following exercise.

Exercise 2.13   Transcribe the following words:

1. Yale, yak, yen, yield, yoke, yacht, yawl, yule
2. hue, hew, human, view, cute
3. beautiful, onion, music, accurate
4. news, tune, yolk, fugue
5. moose, mousse, moos, muse, mews

[ŋ] (eng)

The symbol [ŋ] represents the sound of *ng* in *sang* [sæŋ] and *n* in *sank* [sæŋk]. Note that in the combination *ng*, *g* is sometimes pronounced, sometimes not, for example, *finger* ['fɪŋgɚ], *singer* ['sɪŋɚ].

Exercise 2.14   Transcribe the following words:

1. long, longer, lung, fungus, sunk
2. hung, hunger, sing, tingling
3. dunk, monk, blink, conquer
4. tango, concord, ingrate, pancake

[ʃ] (esh)
[ʒ] (ezh or tailed Z)

The symbol [ʃ] represents the sound of *sh* in *shot* [ʃat] or *ti* of the syllable *-tion*, as in *nation* ['neɪʃən]. The symbol [ʒ] represents the sound of *s* in *pleasure* ['plɛʒɚ] or *si* in *Asia* ['eɪʒə]. Both sounds have other spellings, which are illustrated in the following exercise.

Exercise 2.15   Transcribe the following words:

1. shad, shade, shed, shod, should, shied
2. passion, machine, fiction, fashion
3. fascist, sugar, issue, ocean, special
4. confusion, occasion, decision, prestige, garage
5. fusion, fission, concussion, glacier, glazier

Exercise 2.16   Read the following transcriptions aloud, then write the words they represent.

1. ['mɛʒɚ, 'mouʃən, ɹʌʃ, ɹæʃ, ɹuz, ɹuʒ]
2. ['liʒɚ, blʌʃ, beɪʒ, 'feɪʃəl, ɪn'fleɪʃən]
3. ['siʃɛl, ʃɪp, ʃeɪp, ʃɪp, ʃɑp, ɹ'ɹouʒən]
4. [hʌʃ, wɪŋz, ɪm'pɹɛst, bə'ɹɑʒ]

[tʃ, dʒ]   The combined symbol [tʃ] represents the sound of *ch* in *chat* [tʃæt]; [dʒ] represents the sound of *j* in *joy* [dʒɔɪ]. Both sounds have other spellings. These combined consonant sounds are called *affricates*. (See Chapter 3.)

Exercise 2.17   Transcribe the following words:

1. chants, choke, choice, cheek
2. catch, ketch, cello, baggage
3. jam, judge, bridge, gem
4. batch, badge, just, gust, gist, jest
5. char, jar, ridge, rich

[ɾ] (fish-hook R)   The symbol [ɾ] is used to represent the sound of *r* in the stereotypical English butler's "very ['vɛɾɪ] good, sir." The sound, which is also represented by *rr*, is called a *one-tap trill*. The American articulation of *t, tt* as well as *d, dd* between vowels is very similar to [ɾ]; thus, *catty* and *caddy* might be pronounced ['kæɾɪ], although convention dictates that we transcribe *t* or *tt* as [t] and *d* or *dd* as [d].

One position in which some Americans use the pronunciation [ɾ] for *r* is after *th*. If the words *three, throw* are pronounced quickly and forcefully, the *r* can become a one-tap trill.

[θ] (theta)
[ð] (eth—
pronounced [εð])

The symbol [θ] represents the sound of *th* in *thin* [θɪn]. The symbol [ð] represents the sound of *th* in *then* [ðɛn].

Exercise 2.18   Transcribe the following words:

1. this, that, think, thin
2. thrift, three, brother, bother
3. wrath, rather, cloth, clothing
4. path, paths, south, southern
5. throng, faith, Gothic, father

Exercise 2.19   Read the following transcriptions aloud, then write the words they represent. Some may have more than one spelling:

1. ['weɪdʒɚ, wɪtʃ, 'ʃepɚd, 'ɹetʃɪd, ɹɛkt]
2. [heɪld, 'twaɪˌlaɪt, ɛk'spɪɹɪəns, 'pɹɑmptlɪ]
3. ['fɛðɚ, ə'nʌðɚ, 'tʃɑɹmɪŋ, ɹeɪndʒ, tʌŋz]
4. [juθ, dʒus, mauðz, hɛlθ, 'θʌndəɹəs]
5. [stɹɛtʃ, 'fɹeɪɡɹənt, 'stɛlθɪ, bauz]
6. [θɹɛd, θɹʌst, 'blasəmz, mɪst, 'buzəm]
7. ['paɪəs, 'pɹɪði, 'eɪndʒəl, ɪɹ'dʒɔɪs]
8. [ˌfæɹ'wɛl, sɔŋz, 'θauzənd, 'ɹʌʃɪŋ, dʒu'dɪʃəs]
9. [ðaɪn, tɪtʃ, haɪt, eɪk, 'nʌθɪŋ, mjut]
10. ['ɑɹtʃɪz, dɛpθ, bouθ, tʃɔɪs, ðou]

Describing Sounds: Articulatory Phonetics

When learning the sounds of another language, it is useful to describe the mechanical means by which sounds are formed. If a sound is articulated differently from its English analog, what do we do with the different parts of our vocal apparatus to reflect this difference? The study of how sounds are produced is called articulatory phonetics.

It is logical to begin the study of articulatory phonetics by analyzing the sounds of one's own language, as the student can produce the sounds naturally and can then determine by feel how the speech apparatus is being employed to produce them. Having thus become consciously aware of the speech apparatus, the student can learn to control it and use it to produce unfamiliar sounds.

The main objective of this chapter is to make you aware of how you use your speech apparatus to produce sounds. Appendix A contains charts that provide complete phonetic descriptions of each vowel and consonant.

CONSONANTS

A consonant is a sound in which the airflow is constricted or stopped. A fairly complete description of the production of a consonant sound can be given with three items of information:

1. voicing
2. major articulators
3. manner of production

The sound [b], for example, is described as a *voiced bilabial stop.*

Voicing

When the vocal cords vibrate during the production of a sound, for example [z], the sound is said to be voiced. When they do not vibrate, as in the production of [s], the sound is said to be voiceless.

Exercise 3.1   Indicate whether the underlined letters in the following words represent voiced or voiceless consonants. Refer to the chart in Appendix A only to check yourself.

1. <u>t</u>on	12. pat<u>s</u>
2. <u>d</u>en	13. pad<u>s</u>
3. be<u>d</u>	14. boxe<u>s</u>
4. be<u>t</u>	15. vi<u>si</u>on
5. <u>p</u>ad	16. mi<u>ss</u>ion
6. <u>b</u>ad	17. e<u>dg</u>e
7. hi<u>s</u>	18. e<u>tch</u>
8. thi<u>s</u>	19. ra<u>g</u>
9. thi<u>s</u>tle	20. ra<u>ck</u>
10. ba<u>th</u>	21. <u>w</u>in
11. ba<u>ths</u>	

Articulators

The second of the three items used in the description of a consonant sound indicates the major articulators involved in its production. Below is a list of such terms. Figure 3–1 identifies the main apparatus for producing speech sounds.

Bilabial

A bilabial consonant involves the use of both lips to stop or constrict the flow of breath, for example, [b] or [w].

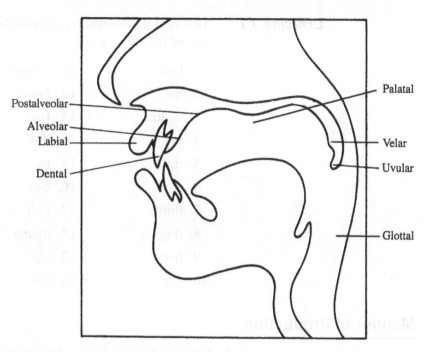

Figure 3–1. Points of articulation.

Labiodental

A labiodental consonant involves the upper teeth and lower lip in its production, for example, [f].

Dental

In articulating a dental consonant, the tip of the tongue is brought into contact with the back of the upper teeth, as in [θ].

Alveolar

An alveolar consonant involves the tip or blade of the tongue and the alveolar ridge in its production, as in [n], [z].

Postalveolar

A postalveolar consonant involves the tip or blade of the tongue and the area above the alveolar ridge, for example, [ʃ].

Palatal

A palatal consonant is produced with the blade of the tongue and the hard palate, as in [j].

Velar

A velar consonant is formed with the back of the tongue and the velum, or soft palate, for example, [k] or [ŋ].

Glottal

The glottis is the opening between the vocal cords. It is almost closed in the production of the glottal consonant [h].

Exercise 3.2 Describe the sounds represented by the underlined letters with one of the above terms.

1. ball	11. mission
2. cat	12. laser
3. vision	13. find
4. nut	14. thin
5. tip	15. ton
6. wolf	16. bad
7. think	17. volt
8. dog	18. mama
9. hot	19. sip
10. yes	20. this

Manner of Production

In the preceding section we discussed the apparatus involved in producing speech sounds. We now need to describe how the apparatus is used to produce the sounds. Although [t] and [s] may both be described as alveolar and voiceless, it is clear that we are using the same apparatus to do two quite different things.

Below is a list of terms that describe the manner in which consonant sounds are produced.[1]

Stop

In the production of a stop, the airflow is stopped momentarily by a set of articulators and then released, as in [b] or [k]. Stops are also called *plosives*.

Fricative

A fricative is the type of sound produced by directing the airflow past a set of articulators without stopping it, but narrowing the space between the articulators to create friction, as in [s], [v], or [θ].[2]

---

[1]Additional terminology:
Aspiration: Aspiration generally refers to the puff of air that follows a consonant such as [p, t, k] in English or German. In the Romance languages, this aspiration is usually absent.
Liquid: The consonants *l* and *r* are sometimes referred to as liquids, regardless of articulation.
[2]Fricatives are also sometimes called *spirants*. The s-like fricatives [s], [z], [ʃ], and [ʒ] are occasionally referred to as *sibilants*.

Affricate

An affricate is a consonant sound consisting of two sounds spoken rapidly together, for example, [tʃ] and [dʒ]. An affricate consists of a stop that is released as a fricative.

Nasal

In the production of a nasal, the flow of air is directed through the nasal passages, as in [m] or [ŋ].

Lateral

In the production of a lateral, the airflow is directed over the sides of the tongue, as in [l].

Glide

The English glides are [w] and [j]. Glides are sometimes called *semi-vowels*. They begin with a brief vowel sound—[w] begins with the vowel [u], [j] begins with the vowel [i]—before proceeding to the characteristic consonant sound.

Approximant

In an approximant, the articulators approach each other but do not interrupt or restrict the airflow as with a stop or a fricative. The pronunciation [ɹ] for the letter *r* is an approximant.[3] Glides can also be classified as approximants.

Trill

A trill is the rapid contact between the tip of the tongue and the alveolar ridge or between the uvula and the back of the tongue. In classical singing, only the former type is considered. English has only the one-tap trill [ɾ]. In other languages, notably Italian, this [ɾ] may be trilled a number of times in rapid succession, producing the trill [r].[4]

---

[3]Depending in part on the sounds surrounding it, the pronunciation of *r* in American English can vary between [ɹ], which the IPA describes as a "voiced dental or alveolar approximant," and [ɻ], which the IPA describes as a "voiced retroflex approximant." In a retroflex articulation, the tip of the tongue is curled upward, and perhaps backward, sometimes nearly to the hard palate.

[4]Many sources use the symbol [r] to indicate various types of articulation, depending on the language and the intended audience.

Exercise 3.3   Using the above terms, give the manner of production for the sounds represented by the underlined letters.

1. pot
2. school
3. vat
4. that
5. man
6. sank
7. fin
8. mission
9. kitchen
10. chair

11. vision
12. blizzard
13. rash
14. thrash
15. fun
16. dug
17. bell
18. yet
19. wolf
20. rigid

Exercise 3.4   Write the IPA symbol for the sounds described as follows:

1. voiced bilabial stop
2. voiced dental fricative
3. voiceless velar stop
4. voiced alveolar nasal
5. voiced palatal glide
6. voiceless alveolar fricative

Exercise 3.5   Give complete, three-part descriptions of the sounds represented by the underlined letters.

1. spot
2. myth
3. tub
4. think
5. dim
6. wet
7. visible

8. fish
9. fusion
10. bell
11. very
12. feel
13. dog
14. dot

VOWELS

The word *vowel* comes from the Latin *vocalis*, meaning "related to the voice" (The German word for *vowel* is *Vokal* [voˈkaːl]). Vowels are voiced sounds that are produced without restricting or stopping the breath as most consonants do.

Vowel Description

Tongue

In the pronunciation of vowels, the tongue is usually in an arched position with the tip pointing down. Although the entire tongue changes position in pronouncing different vowels, it is convenient to use the position of the peak, or highest point, of the tongue arch in describing vowel sounds. Figure 3–2 shows the shape of the arch for certain vowels, with the dot indicating the position of the peak for each. This group of vowels, [i, e, ɛ, a] and [u, o. ɔ, ɑ], is known as the *primary cardinal vowels*.

If we now consider the peaks alone, we see that they can be arranged schematically, as in Figure 3–3. From Figures 3–2 and 3–3 it can be seen that [i, e, ɛ, a][5] are arranged roughly along a sloping line toward the front of the mouth and that [u, o, ɔ, ɑ][5] are arranged roughly along a less sharply sloping line toward the back of the mouth, the whole configuration suggesting the form of a quadrilateral that has [i, a, ɑ, u] as its corners (Figure 3–4). For the sake of reference, it is convenient to arrange the vowels within or along the boundaries of a trapezoid, as in Figure 3–5. (See also Appendix A, Chart 3.)

From Figure 3–5, we see that we can pinpoint the position of the peak of the arched tongue in somewhat the same manner as we locate a point on a grid, by giving its horizontal position (front, central, back) and its vertical position (high, mid, low). Thus we see that [i] may be described as a *high front vowel*.

---

[5]Recall that the sounds [e, a, o] occur generally in standard American English only in the diphthongs [eɪ, aɪ, aʊ, oʊ] or in some unstressed syllables.

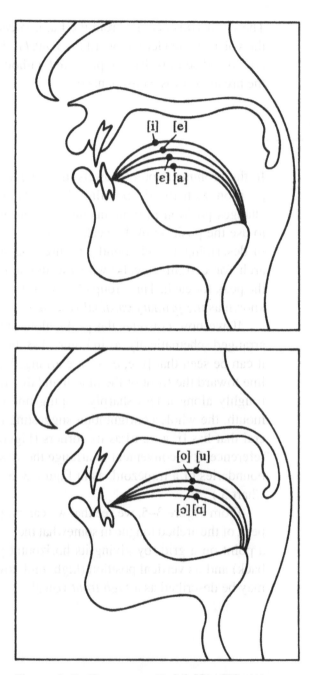

Figure 3–2. Tongue position for vowels.

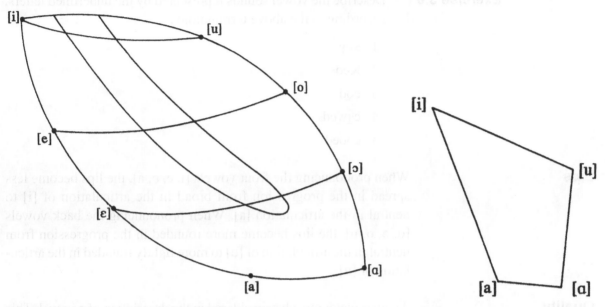

Figure 3–3. Schematic position of primary cardinal vowels.

Figure 3–4. Vowel quadrilateral.

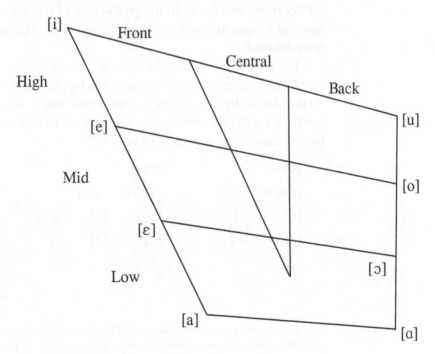

Figure 3–5. Primary cardinal vowels.

Exercise 3.6   Describe the vowel sounds represented by the underlined letters, according to the above terminology.

1. ke*y*ed
2. K*e*ds
3. c*o*d
4. c*aw*ed
5. c*oo*ed

Lips

When pronouncing the front vowels [i, e, ɛ, a], the lips become less spread in the progression from broad in the articulation of [i] to neutral in the articulation [a]. When pronouncing the back vowels [ɑ, ɔ, o, u], the lips become more rounded in the progression from neutral in the articulation of [ɑ] to more tightly rounded in the articulation of [u].

Quality

Another factor must be considered in the description of a vowel. This is known as tension or closeness. The difference between [i] and [ɪ], for example, lies not only in the fact that for [ɪ], the tongue is drawn farther down and back. In the production of [i], the muscles of the lips and tongue are under tension. With [ɪ], the lips and tongue are more relaxed.

The vowel [i] is said to be *tense* or *closed;* the vowel [ɪ] is *lax* or *open.* The contrast can be felt physically by placing the finger lightly on the chin or by placing the thumb on the tongue muscle under the lower jaw and pronouncing the two sounds in succession. The following are contrasting pairs of vowels[6]:

Front		Back	
closed	*open*	*closed*	*open*
[i]	[ɪ]	[u]	[ʊ]
[e]	[ɛ]	[o]	[ɔ]

---

[6]The IPA uses the term *close* (pronounced [kloʊs]), and describes these vowels as follows: [i] is close, [ɪ] is near-close; [u] is close, [ʊ] is near-close; [e] is close, [ɛ] is open; [o] is close, [ɔ] is open.

Exercise 3.7   Identify the vowels in the following words as closed or open. (For the diphthongs, identify the initial, or dominant, vowel.)

1. wooed, would, full, fool, push
2. hole, hall, code, cawed, home
3. bet, bait. wade, wed, peg
4. seat, sit. list. leased, seize
5. frost, pose, pill, do, vault

PART II

The Sounds of German

Introduction

In many respects, German is an easy language to pronounce for speakers of English. It is commonly said to be a "phonetic" language; that is, for each spelling there are normally no more than one or two pronunciations, and, conversely, for each pronunciation there are usually no more than one or two spellings. Contrast this situation with English, which has, as we pointed out in Chapter 1, at least ten spellings for the sound [i] and at least six pronunciations for the letter *a*.

Even when there are two pronunciations for a letter in German, it is fairly easy for the singer to recognize from the position of the letter in the word, and from the letters following it, which pronunciation is to be chosen. In some instances, it will be necessary to recognize certain prefixes or verb endings in order to choose the right pronunciation.

ORGANIZATION

Since German is a fairly phonetic language, and since one of the singer's main objectives in a study of German diction is to learn to pronounce German words printed in a score, the arrangement in this book is based on *spellings*—written symbols—rather than on sounds. Thus, even though *c* and *z* or *ie* and *i* may sometimes be pronounced alike, they are treated in different sections.

This text departs from the traditional approach of treating vowels and consonants completely separately. It instead treats the letters and

31

their pronunciations in the order of decreasing difficulty. The difficult consonants *ch* and *r* are treated first, then the difficult closed and open vowels. The treatment of vowels is followed by a discussion of word structure, which will facilitate the differentiation of sounds; then concluding chapters on vowels and consonants are presented.

GENERAL RULES

Before beginning a detailed study of German sounds, the singer should become familiar with a few general rules regarding pronunciation and orthography.

Pronunciation Like English

In general, the singer may assume that the following consonants are pronounced as in English: *b, ck, d, f, g, h, k, m, n, p, t, x*. Exceptions will be discussed under the individual consonants.

Double Consonants

In German, double consonants are generally pronounced the same as single consonants, as in *beginnen* [bə'gɪnən] "begin."[1]

Unvoicing

The voiced consonants *b, d, g, s* are usually unvoiced in final position or before a consonant, for instance, *d* in *Bad* [baːt] "bath," *g* in *legt* [leːkt] "lays."

Word Structure

The division of words into their component parts can affect vowel quality and unvoicing, as well as the pronunciation of double consonants and consonant clusters. Word structure is discussed further in Chapter 7.

---

[1]Some singers may extend the consonant, depending on expressive intention.

Capitalization

The student will note that many words in the following examples and exercises are capitalized. In German, all nouns are capitalized, including common nouns such as *Winter, Musik*, and the like.

Umlaut

The umlaut letters ä, ö, ü are also spelled *ae, oe, ue* in some scores. There is no difference in pronunciation. Many words containing these letters have related forms without umlaut, for example, *Hand* "hand," *Hände* "hands"; *backen* "bake," *bäckt* "bakes."

Stress

In words of Germanic origin, the stress is generally on the first syllable: *Winter* ['vɪntɐ] "winter," *mitkommen* ['mɪtˌkɔmən] "come along." In words containing the prefixes *be-, ent-, er-, ge-, ver-, zer-*, the next syllable will be stressed, as in *beginnen* [bə'gɪnən] "begin." In this book, stress will not be indicated for words that follow these two stress patterns. If the stress falls on a different syllable, it will be indicated, as in *Mu'sik, Or'chester*. There are many German words borrowed from other languages in which the stress usually falls on the final syllable, as in *ele'gant* [ele'gant] "elegant." (See Chapter 7 for a more detailed discussion of stress.)

REFERENCE WORKS

Siebs

For many years, the definitive reference work, designed for use by professional actors, singers, and announcers, was *Deutsche Aussprache* ("German Pronunciation") by Theodor Siebs, published by Walter de Gruyter & Co. Although it is now out of print, the last edition (19th, 1969) is available in print-on-demand or e-book format. Siebs provides pronunciations in IPA transcription of most German words and foreign words commonly found in German, as well as transcriptions of a large number of proper names.

Duden

Another valuable reference is *Das Aussprachewörterbuch* ("The Pronunciation Dictionary"), Volume 6 in the twelve-volume Duden series which covers many aspects of the German language. Like Siebs, Duden provides IPA transcriptions of German words, foreign words commonly found in German, and proper names.

In previous editions, *German for Singers* generally followed Siebs. In this edition, we have made several changes that reflect current usage in Duden and other sources. These changes are frequently supported by comments made by Siebs in the introduction to *Deutsche Aussprache*, as we will note.

There are many other works that contain IPA transcriptions; but we feel that, because of their concise nature and their long history, Siebs and Duden are the most convenient and useful references for the singer.

5

The Sounds of *r, ch*

We want to begin the treatment of German pronunciation with the difficult consonants *r* and *ch*. The exercises in subsequent chapters can then include these consonants and provide ongoing practice in their articulation. We review and conclude the treatment of the sounds of this chapter in Chapters 12 and 15.

SECTION 1: *r, rr* Part I   (See Chapter 12 for Continuation.)

Speaking Versus Singing

In speaking, the pronunciation of *r* before a vowel is uvular in many German-speaking areas; that is, it involves contact between the far back part of the tongue and the uvula, producing a slight gargling sound. The uvular pronunciation (IPA [ʁ]) is used in singing popular songs but should be avoided in art songs and opera. The one-tap trill or flipped *r* (IPA [ɾ]) should be used instead.

In other positions, the pronunciation of *r* in speaking is more vowel-like in quality. The conditions for the use of this latter pronunciation in singing are not as clearly defined as those for most German sounds, and the singer is left a certain amount of latitude in its use. We will provide guidelines that should give the singer a good basis for learning the pronunciation of *r* in German.

Prevocalic

[ɾ] (One-tap trill, or flipped *r*)

The letter *r* should generally be pronounced as a one-tap trill, also called flipped *r*, when it comes before a vowel:[1] *raten* [ˈraːtən] "guess," *beraten* [bəˈraːtən] "advise." The singer should take care to tap the tongue only once against the lower part of the alveolar ridge.[2]

In general, the articulation of *rr* in one element is the same as that for *r: Karre* [ˈkaɾə] "cart."

Note: Recall from the General Rules in Chapter Four: (1) Stress is on the first syllable except after be-, ent-, er-, ge-, ver-, zer-; (2) Consonants are unvoiced at the end of an element.

Exercise 5.1

Pronounce the following words, observing the rules for the pronunciation of *r* and *rr*.

1. Rand	3. aufragen
rasch	Abreise
Rest	Hauptrolle
retten	bereue
ringen	gerissen
Reigen	
rauschen	
Reue	
2. Karre	4. fragen
irren	Kragen
fahren	tragen
ihren	dreist
sperren	graben
führen	Preis
lauere	Schrift
eure	bringen

---

[1] In spoken German, it is pronounced this way in parts of Austria, Switzerland, and southern Germany.

[2] Note: 2 to 3 tap trill [r] (IPA name: lower-case R)

In some prevocalic positions, the articulation of *r* or *rr* may be extended to two or three taps for expressive purposes. The IPA symbol for this two- to three-tap trill is [r]. Since we discourage the use of this trill at first, and since the symbol [r] often appears in dictionaries and other sources to stand for a variety of pronunciations for the letter *r*, it will not be used in this book. We recommend only sparing use of this extended trill, to be undertaken after consultation with experienced singers and coaches.

Exercise 5.2　Read the following excerpt:

| Lass irre Hunde heulen, vor ihres Herren Haus... | Let mad dogs howl before their master's house... |

Winterreise
Müller/Schubert

Final Position in Some Words and Word Elements: [ɐ̯], [ɐ]³ (turned A)

The other pronunciation of *r* is, in effect, a vowel sound that can be viewed as a variant of the schwa sound [ə]. The tongue is drawn back a little farther than for schwa and the lips are slightly rounded, producing a vowel that is very close to the sound of *o* in the British pronunciation of the word *hot*.

[ɐ̯]

We will use the symbol [ɐ̯] to designate this vocalic articulation of *r* when it appears after a vowel, as in *mir* [miːɐ̯] *"me."*⁴ (The diacritic beneath the symbol, called "subscript arch," indicates that the sound is nonsyllabic—that is, it is part of the preceding syllable, not a separate syllable.) In the articulation of schwa, the tip of the tongue is normally pointed down; in the articulation of [ɐ̯], the tongue should be pointed at, but not touching, the alveolar ridge. In this manner, the relationship of [ɐ̯] to the one-tap trill [ɾ] is maintained, and the articulations may be easily interchanged as style may require.

There are no hard and fast rules regarding the use of [ɐ̯]. Indeed, some singers almost never use it. However, most singers now make judicious use of [ɐ̯], especially in the nineteenth-century art song.

---

³Some references do not differentiate between the two types of *r*, using the symbol [r] for both. However, the singer is urged to adopt [ɾ] as well as [ɐ̯], [ɐ] in making phonetic notations in order to reflect the difference in articulation.

⁴Siebs uses [ʁ] to indicate a *uvular* articulation. In general, however, the symbol appears in the Siebs entries in the same positions described here; the singer need only remember to use the more vocalic articulation [ɐ̯].

As a rule of thumb, let us say that *r* will be pronounced [ɐ̯] in the following cases:

1. the article *der* [deːɐ̯] "the"

2. the pronouns
   mir [miːɐ̯] "me"
   dir [diːɐ̯] "you"
   er [eːɐ̯] "he"
   ihr [iːɐ̯] "her," "their," "you,"
   wir [viːɐ̯] "we"
   wer [veːɐ̯] "who"

3. the prepositions
   für [fyːɐ̯] "for"
   vor [foːɐ̯] "before"

4. the prefixes
   er- [ɛɐ̯]
   ver- [fɛɐ̯]
   zer- [tsɛɐ̯]

5. generally after a long vowel, as in
   Bier [biːɐ̯] "beer"
   werden [ˈveːɐ̯dən] "become"

[ɐ]: Final *-er*; Syllabic *-er-*

In general, final *-er* is pronounced [ɐ], as in *guter* [ˈɡutɐ] "good." Because *-er* constitutes its own syllable, the subscript arch is not used.

The suffix *-er* is pronounced [ɐ], as in *bitter* [ˈbɪtɐ] "bitter." This suffix may also occur before other suffixes, or endings beginning with consonants, as in *bitterster* [ˈbɪtɐstɐ] "bitterest," or in verb forms such as *flattern* [ˈflatɐn] "flutter," *wandern* [ˈvandɐn] "wander."

[The suffix *-er* should not be confused with the prefix *er-*, which is always pronounced [ɛɐ̯], as in *erfahren* [ɛɐ̯ˈfaːrən] "experience."]

In the previous section, we noted that the symbol [ɐ̯] is used to indicate an *approximation* of an *r*-sound. In the case of the suffix *-er,* it is being used to represent the combined sound of a schwa and an *r*. Duden and others render *Vater* "father" as [ˈfaːtɐ]. Siebs, however, gives only ['fɑːtər] and ['fɑːtɐʁ], reflecting both the vowel and the *r*, as either a trill or a voiceless uvular fricative. The singer can bear in mind that, in German diction, the symbols [ɐ̯] and [ɐ] are vowel sounds, but imply an *r* sound, which the singer can decide to articulate as flipped *r*, depending on the context.

Other Positions: [ɾ]

In positions other than those described above, *r, rr* should be pronounced as the one-tap trill [ɾ] (see also Chapter 12), for example:

1. *r* + consonant after a short vowel: *warten* ['vaɾtən] "wait"
2. *rr: Herr* [hɛɾ] "gentleman," *irrt* [ɪɾt] "errs"

Rule of Thumb
For Pronouncing *r*

Vocalic *r*

[ɐ̯]

- when final: mi*r* [miːɐ̯], Bie*r* [biːɐ̯], e*r*kennen [ɛɐ̯ˈkɛnən]

- preconsonantal after a long vowel: we*r*den ['veːɐ̯dən]

[ɐ]

- for final -*er:* Vat*er* ['faːtɐ]

Flipped *r* [ɾ]

- before a vowel: *r*aten ['ɾaːtən], f*r*agen ['fɾaːgən], be*r*aten [bəˈɾaːtən], fah*r*en ['faːɾən]

- *rr* in all positions: Ka*rr*e ['kaɾə], He*rr* [hɛɾ], i*rr*en ['ɪɾən], i*rr*t [ɪɾt]

- preconsonantal after a short vowel: wa*r*ten ['vaɾtən]

Exercise 5.3

Pronounce the following words, using [ɐ̯] or [ɐ] for *r, er* in the recommended words and syllables:

1. der, wer, mir, ihr, wir

2. erfahren, erkennen, verkleiden, der'selbe, versagen

3. Lieder, leider, Vater, Meistersinger, Wagner, Wiener, immer, besser, Musiker, Or'chester, Walter, Ritter, Retter, Wunder, Kindergarten

4. wandern, wanderst, wandert, wanderten, verbessert, mildert, flatterte, bitterlich

Exercise 5.4

Final *e* is pronounced as schwa [ə] in German (see Chapter 6, Section 3). Practice contrasting [ə] and [ɐ] in the following pairs:

1. Messe	Messer
2. spiele	Spieler
3. gute	guter
4. Liede	Lieder
5. Leide	leider
6. Liebe	lieber
7. Treue	treuer
8. meiste	Meister
9. blaue	blauer

Exercise 5.5

Transcribe the following words into the IPA, using [ɾ] or [ɐ], [ɐ̯]:

1. Lieder, Bier, Rest, Retter, Kraft

2. Ritter, wandern, irren, Schubert, Bruckner

Excerpt

Read the following passage aloud, paying special attention to the pronunciation of *r*:

So wie dort in blauer Tiefe,	Just as there in blue depths,
Hell und herrlich, jener Stern,	brilliant and magnificent, that star,
Also er an meinem Himmel,	so (is) he in *my* heaven,
Hell und herrlich, hehr und fern.	brilliant and magnificent, noble and distant.

Frauenliebe und -leben
Chamisso/Schumann

SECTION 2: *ch* PART I (See Chapter 15 for Continuation)

There are two distinctly different pronunciations of *ch.*

[x] (lower-case X)

The sound [x] is a voiceless velar fricative, a heavily aspirated [h], as in *Bach* [bax]. This pronunciation of *ch* occurs after the back vowels *a, o, u, au.* It is commonly referred to in German as the *ach-Laut* ("ach-sound").[5]

Exercise 5.6

Pronounce the following words, using [x] for *ch:*

1. ach, machen, Pracht, Nacht, gemacht
2. Loch, noch, doch
3. auch, Rauch, Raucher
4. Buch, Kuchen, suchen

[ç] (C cedilla)

The sound [ç] is a voiceless palatal fricative. It is commonly referred to in German as the *ich-Laut* ("ich-sound"). For [ç], the tongue is in the same position as for [j], but air is passed over it, producing a hissing sound. The sound is very much like the initial sound in the English words *hue, huge, and human,* as pronounced in standard American English. Except after the back vowels *a, o, u and au,* the pronunciation of *ch* is [ç].

Other pronunciations for *ch* are treated in the conclusion of the discussion of *ch* in Chapter 15.

Exercise 5.7

Pronounce the following words, using [ç] for *ch:*

1. rächen, Becher, brechen, riechen, ich, mich
2. nicht, Angesicht, schleichen, Eiche, euch, feucht
3. mancher, Milch, welcher, Kelch
4. schnarchen, Lerche, Liebchen, Männchen

---

[5]The IPA Handbook describes two types of *ach-Laut:* [χ], a voiceless uvular fricative, which occurs after low back vowels (e.g. *Bach* [baχ] "brook," *doch* [dɔχ] "yet") and [x], a voiceless velar fricative used after high and mid back tense vowels (e.g. *Buch* [bux] "book," *hoch* [hox] "high"). Most references do not reflect this distinction in transcription.

Exercise 5.8   Transcribe the following words into the IPA ($ä = [ɛ]$):

1. ich, ach, Becher, nicht, Milch
2. Nacht, Nächte, Bach, Bäche

Excerpt   Read the following passage aloud, paying special attention to the pronunciation of *ch*.

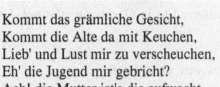

Kommt das grämliche Gesicht,	Is that a grouchy face coming,
Kommt die Alte da mit Keuchen,	is the old lady coming, with (her) wheezing,
Lieb' und Lust mir zu verscheuchen,	to chase (away) my love and pleasure
Eh' die Jugend mir gebricht?	before my youth is over?
Ach! die Mutter ist's die aufwacht,	Oh! It's Mother, who's waking up
Und den Mund zu schelten aufmacht,	and opening her mouth to scold.
Nein, die Karten lügen nicht!	No, the cards don't lie!

Die Kartenlegerin
Chamisso/Schumann

Recording

Practice speaking the text of the following song until you can read it through without errors. Then record the text, without pausing; if you make a mistake, start over.

Note: initial st = [ʃt]; z = [ts].

Am Brunnen vor dem Tore,	At the fountain before the city gate,
Da steht ein Lindenbaum,	there stands a linden tree;
Ich träumt' in seinem Schatten	I have dreamt in its shade
So manchen süßen Traum.	so many a sweet dream.
Ich schnitt in seine Rinde	I carved into its bark
So manches liebe Wort,	so many a sweet word,
Es zog in Freud' und Leide	I felt drawn in joy and sorrow
Zu ihm mich immer fort.	to it again and again.
Ich musst' auch heute wandern	Today too, I had to walk
Vorbei in tiefer Nacht,	past (it) deep in the night,
Da hab' ich noch im Dunkeln	then, still in darkness, I
Die Augen zugemacht;	closed my eyes;
Und seine Zweige rauschten	and its branches rustled
Als riefen sie mir zu:	as if they were calling to me:
Komm her zu mir Geselle,	Come here to me, companion,
Hier find'st du deine Ruh.	here you will find your peace.
Die kalten Winde bliesen	The cold winds were blowing
Mir grad' ins Angesicht;	right into my face;
Der Hut flog mir vom Kopfe,	my hat flew off my head,
Ich wendete mich nicht.	I did not turn around.
Nun bin ich manche Stunde	Now I am many an hour
Entfernt von jenem Ort,	distant from that place,
Und immer hör' ich's rauschen:	and I always hear it rustling:
Du fändest Ruhe dort.	You would find peace there.

Song   Sing the following song. Pay careful attention to the contrasts [ɾ]
: [ɐ̯], [ɐ] and [x] : [ç]

Am Brunnen vor dem Tore

Am Brun - nen vor dem To - re   da steht ein Lin - den -
Ich mußt' auch heu - te wan - dern   vor - bei in tie - fer
Die kal - ten Win - de blie - sen   mir grad' ins An - ge -

baum, ich träumt' in sein - em Schat - ten so man - chen sü - ßen
Nacht, da hab' ich noch im Dun - keln die Au - gen zu - ge -
sicht; der Hut flog mir vom Kop - fe, ich wen - de - te____ mich

Traum; ich schnitt in sei - ne Rin - de so man - ches lie - be
macht; und sei - ne Zwei - ge rausch - ten als rie - fen sie mir
nicht. Nun bin ich man - che Stun - de ent - fernt von je - nem

Wort, es zog in Freud' und Lei - de zu
zu: Komm her zu mir Ge - sel - le, hier
Ort, und im - mer hör' ich's rau - schen: Du

ihm ___ mich im - mer fort, zu ihm ___ mich im - mer fort.
find'st ___ du dei - ne Ruh, hier find'st ___ du dei - ne Ruh.
fän - dest Ru - he dort, du fän - dest Ru - he dort.

6

Monophthongs—Part One: Long and Closed or Short and Open

Certain monophthongs are generally *either* long and closed *or* short and open. This group consists of *i*, *ü* (and *y*), *e*, *ö*, *o*, and *u*.

The vowels *a*, *ä*, and, as a general rule, *ie*, are also monophthongs; however, since they do not reflect the same patterns of length and quality as the vowels of this chapter, they are not discussed here (see Chapter 9).[1]

DIPHTHONGIZATION

In Chapter 2, it was pointed out that the English vowels generally assumed to be monophthongs frequently have a diphthongal element. This is generally true of the vowels commonly referred to as "long *a*" [eɪ] and "long *o*"[oʊ]. It is also true of other vowels to a greater or lesser extent, depending on regional accent. One frequently hears reference to the "purity" of vowels in European languages. By this "purity" is meant the absence of the diphthongal elements characteristic

---

[1]Because these vowels will appear in some examples and exercises, note that they are generally transcribed as follows: *a*=[a, aː], *ä*=[ɛ, ɛː], *ie*=[iː]. Examples: *Manne* ['manə] "man," *mahne* ['maːnə] "(I) warn"; *Männer* ['mɛnɐ] "men," *Mähne* ['mɛːnə] "mane"; *Miene* ['miːnə] "mien (look, expression)."

47

of some English vowels. Thus, the pronunciation of the English word *Dane* [deɪn] is by no means the same as that for the German word *den* [deːn] "the."

Practice the contrast between English and German vowels in the following pairs of words. You will note that for the English diphthong sounds, the jaw moves slightly during the pronunciation of the vowel. For the German sound, concentrate on holding the jaw in one position while articulating the vowel.

Exercise 6.1   Contrast:

English	German	
1. bate	Beet	"flowerbed"
2. lame	Lehm	"mud"
3. lone	Lohn	"wage"
4. tote	tot	"dead"
5. toot	tut	"does"
6. geese	gieß	"pour"
7. puts	Putz	"finery"
8. bet	Bett	"bed"
9. pest	Pest	"pestilence"
10. mitt	mit	"with"
11. bin	bin	"am"

QUALITY

In Chapter 3, we discussed the distinction between closed, tense vowels and open, lax vowels. The monophthongs discussed in this chapter—*i*, *ü* (and *y*), *e*, *ö*, *o*, u—will be long and closed in some positions and short and open in others.

LENGTH

In spoken German, a long vowel is actually extended to about double the duration of a short vowel. In singing, of course, the length of the vowel is largely determined by the length of the note on which it is sung. However, the composer usually assigns a longer note to a long vowel and a shorter note to a short vowel in order to reflect the difference in length of the spoken vowels.

In the IPA, length is indicated by a long mark placed after the vowel, for example, [iː].[2]

RULES ON LENGTH

The vowels of this chapter—*i*, *ü* (and *y*), *e*, *ö*, *o*, *u* —may be either long and closed or short and open, depending on certain conditions.[3]

A. Long Vowels

The vowels of this chapter are regularly long and closed in the following positions:[4]

1. before a single consonant

Exercise 6.2

Pronounce:

Reben	schuf
Weg	Muse
wider	öde
Boden	übel
bog	

2. before *h* (Normally, the *h* following a stressed vowel is not pronounced, even if it precedes another vowel—see also Chapter 13.)

---

[2]If a vowel appears in an unstressed syllable, its quality is maintained in accordance with the rules, but it is usually shorter in duration; hence the length mark is not used: *zugute* [tsuˈguːtə].

[3]The rules stated here also affect the *length* of *a* and *ä*; but since these two vowels do not follow the same pattern of distinction in quality as the vowels of this chapter, they are treated elsewhere (see Chapter 9).

[4]If a word ends in a stressed vowel, the vowel will generally be long, e.g., *du* [duː] "you," *so* [zoː] "so," *Büro* [byˈroː].

Exercise 6.3   Pronounce:

1. stehlen	2. stehen
ihn	drohen
ohne	Ruhe
Ruhm	Flöhe
stöhnen	Brühe
rühren	

3. when doubled
   Of the vowels in this chapter, only *ee* and *oo* occur doubled.[5]

Exercise 6.4   Pronounce:

Beet

Meer

Boot

Moor

B. Short Vowels

The monophthongs of this chapter are nearly always short and open when followed by more than one consonant.

Exercise 6.5   Pronounce:

denn	bunt
Ring	Hölle
Knospe	Lüfte

Notes

1. Exceptions
   There are common exceptions to the above rules on length. In particular, there are many words in which a vowel is pronounced long before *ch*, *st*, or *r* + a dental. In this book, the exceptions commonly found in song literature are listed

---

[5]The only other vowel that occurs doubled is *aa*, as in *Saal* [zaːl] (see Chapter 9).

under the discussion of each vowel. There are of course other exceptions to be found; however, since none of these exceptions will appear in this book, it will not be necessary to look up any word appearing in the exercises and excerpts once the rules and exceptions have been learned. Even in the large body of vocal literature beyond this text, it will be rare for the singer to encounter a word that does not conform to the rules and exceptions as outlined here.

2. *ß*: The *Eszett* or *scharfes s*
According to the new spelling rules adopted in 1996, the character *ß* (called *Eszett* or *scharfes s*) is to appear only after long vowels (including diphthongs). Since *ß* is a single consonant, this usage conforms to rule 1 above. However, depending on the source and date of the song text, the use of the character *ß* is not consistent. In some texts, it is not used at all, and in others it may appear in alternation with *ss* (see Chapter 10). Because *ß* in some texts appears in alternation with *ss*, and in others *ss* is used in place of *ß*, we will provide lists of common words containing a long vowel before *ß*, as written in accordance with the new spelling rules. The singer should learn to recognize these words, as they may appear in some texts with *ss* instead of *ß*. Because there are so many texts still available that do not reflect the new spelling rule, some of the excerpts and exercises in this book will contain words with an older spelling, and the singer will need to learn the lists of words containing a long vowel which appear in the sections below.

3. Word Structure and Vowel Length
For compound words and words containing prefixes, suffixes, or certain grammatical endings, a basic knowledge of German word structure is necessary in order to recognize whether a vowel is followed by one consonant or more than one consonant. This subject is pursued in some detail in Chapter 7 and should be considered an integral part of these rules concerning length.

As we continue our discussion of German sounds and undertake exercises in pronunciation and transcription, it will be helpful to keep the following rules of thumb in mind.

Rules of Thumb

Vowel Length

A vowel is long:

1. Before a single consonant: *Bibel* [ˈbiːbəl] "Bible"

2. Before *h: gehen* [ˈgeːən] "go"

3. When doubled: *Boot* [boːt] "boat"

A vowel is short:

Before two or more consonants: *Winter* [ˈvɪntɐ] "winter"

Stress

In words of Germanic origin:

1. Stress is on the first syllable: *Winter* [ˈvɪntɐ] "winter," *mitkommen* [ˈmɪtˌkɔmən] "come along"

2. After the prefixes be-, ent-, er-, ge-, ver-, zer-, stress is on the next syllable: *beginnen* [bəˈgɪnən] "begin"

Voicing

b, d, g, and *s* are unvoiced when final in word or element: *Bad* [baːt] "bath," *Tag* [taːk] "day," *als* [als] "when," *abbrechen* [ˈapˌbʁɛçən] "break off"

Pronouncing *r*

Vocalic r [ɐ̯, ɐ]

1. [ɐ̯] when final: *mir* [miːɐ̯] "me," *Bier* [biːɐ̯] "beer," *erkennen* [ɛɐ̯ˈkɛnən] "recognize"

52

2. [ɐ̯] preconsonantal after a long vowel: *werden* [ˈveːɐ̯dən] "become"

3. [ɐ] in final *-er: Vater* [ˈfaːtɐ] "father"

Flipped r [ɾ]

1. before a vowel: *raten* [ˈɾaːtən] "guess," *fragen* [ˈfɾaːgən] "ask," *beraten* [bəˈɾaːtən] "advise," *fahren* [ˈfaːɾən] "travel"

2. *rr* in all positions: *Karre* [ˈkaɾə] "cart," *Herr* [hɛɾ] "gentleman," *irren* [ˈɪɾən] "err," *irrt* [ɪɾt] "errs"

3. preconsonantal after a short vowel: *warten* [ˈvaɾtən] "wait"

SECTION 1: *i*

[iː] (lower-case I)

Long and closed [iː] is pronounced about like *i* in English *machine.* It occurs regularly before a single consonant, as in *mir* [miːɐ̯] "me," or before *h*, as in *ihn* [iːn] "him."

Exercise 6.6   Pronounce:

1. ihm, ihr, ihn, ihnen
2. wider, Titel, Bibel, Tiger
3. mir, wir, Appe'tit, Kre'dit

[ɪ] (small capital I)

Short and open [ɪ] is pronounced about like *i* in English *pick*, but higher in the mouth. It occurs regularly before two or more consonants as in *bist* [bɪst] "are."

Exercise 6.7   Pronounce:

1. bitte, spricht, ich, dich, Kind, ist, bist
2. Wirt, wird, irdisch, irgend, Kirsche, Kirche

Exceptions[6]

1. In certain words, *i* is short before a single consonant. Learn these:

in, im [ɪm, ɪn]	"in, in the"
bin [bɪn]	"am"
mit [mɪt]	"with"
hin [hɪn]	"there"
bis [bɪs]	"until"
April [aˈprɪl]	"April"

2. In some suffixes ending in a single consonant, *i* is always short. Memorize these suffixes:

   -in, e.g. *Studentin* [ʃtuˈdɛntɪn] "female student"

   -nis, e.g. *Finsternis* [ˈfɪnstɐnɪs] "darkness"

   -ig, e.g. *blättrig* [ˈblɛtrɪç] "leafy" (Note: -*ig* is pronounced [ɪç] when final or before a consonant [see Ch. 8, Section 3]).

Exercise 6.8

Pronounce:

1. Stuˈdentin
   Feindin
   Ärztin
   Berˈlinerin
   Engländerin

2. Ärgernis
   Kenntnis
   Gefängnis

3. fertig
   giftig
   Käfig

3. In the final syllable -*ik*, *i* is long if the syllable is stressed and short if unstressed. Learn the following:

Stressed	Unstressed
Musik [muˈziːk]	Chronik [ˈkroːnɪk]
Kritik [kriˈtiːk]	Tragik [ˈtraːɡɪk]
Politik [poliˈtiːk]	Lyrik [ˈlyːrɪk]

---

[6]Many of the exceptions listed in this book may appear in various compounds. For example, *in* also appears in *darin*, *worin*, etc.; *mit* appears in *damit*, *mitgehen*, *mithin*, etc. Except as otherwise noted, the pronunciation of the basic word remains the same.

Exercise 6.9   Differentiate between [iː] and [ɪ] in the following pairs:

1. wider   Widder
2. Lid   litt
3. ihnen   innen
4. Stil   still
5. Mine   Minne
6. Iren   irren

Exercise 6.10   Pronounce the following words, applying the rules for long or short monophthongs:

1. hinter, Mitte, Igel, mir, Hirsch
2. finden, Himmel, ihn, in, bilden, dreckig
3. Stu'dentin, Bibel, Kenntnis, Mine
4. Stil, giftig, hin, Titel, mit, Ire, Irin
5. Musik, Lider, Tragik, Kissen, bin

Exercise 6.11   Transcribe the above words into the IPA. (Note: initial *st*=[ʃt])

Excerpts   Read the following excerpts aloud, paying special attention to the pronunciation of *i:*

1.

Doch bin ich, wie ich bin,	But I am how I am,
Und nimm mich nur hin!	and just take me that way!
Willst du bess're besitzen,	If you want to have better,
So lass dir sie schnitzen.	then have them carved.
Ich bin nun, wie ich bin;	I am, then, how I am;
So nimm mich nur hin.	so take me that way.

Liebhaber in allen Gestalten
Goethe/Schubert

2.

Seit ich ihn gesehen,	Since I (first) saw him,
Glaub' ich blind zu sein;	I think I am blind;
Wo ich hin nur blicke,	wherever I look,
Seh' ich ihn allein.	I see only him.

Frauenliebe und -leben
Chamisso/Schumann

Song

Sing the following song, focusing on the contrast between [iː] and [ɪ]. Note that *ie* is usually pronounced [iː].

Du, du liegst mir im Herzen,	You, you are in my heart,
Du, du liegst mir im Sinn.	you, you are in my mind.
Du, du machst mir viel Schmerzen,	You, you cause me much pain,
Weißt nicht, wie gut ich dir bin.	(you) don't know how fond I am of you.
So, so wie ich dich liebe,	Just, just as I love you,
So, so liebe auch mich	so, so, love me too.
Die, die zärtlichsten Triebe	the, the tenderest feelings
Fühle ich einzig für dich.	I have only for you.
Doch, doch darf ich dir trauen,	But, but can I trust you,
Dir, dir mit leichtem Sinn?	you, you, with (your) carefree spirit?
Du, du kannst auf mich bauen,	You, you can rely on me—
Weißt ja wie gut ich dir bin.	yes, you know how fond I am of you.
Und, und wenn in der Ferne,	And, and when from afar
Mir, mir dein Bild erscheint,	before me your image appears,
Dann, dann wünscht' ich so gerne,	then, then I'd wish so dearly
Dass uns die Liebe vereint.	for love to unite us.

Du, du, liegst mir im Herzen

Du,   du,   liegst mir im Her - zen, du,   du,
So,   so,   wie ich dich lie - be, so,   so,
Doch,   doch,   darf ich dir   trau - en, dir,   dir,
Und,   und,   wenn in der   Fer - ne mir,   mir

liegst mir im Sinn.   Du,   du,   machst mir viel Schmer-zen,
lie - be auch mich.   Die, die   zärt - lich-sten Trie - be
mit leich-tem Sinn?   Du,   du,   kannst auf mich bau - en,
dein Bild er - scheint, dann, dann, wünscht' ich so ger - ne,

weißt nicht wie gut ich dir bin.____   Ja, ja,
füh - le ich ein - zig für dich.____   Ja, ja,
weißt ja wie gut ich dir bin.____   Ja, ja,
daß uns die Lie - be ver - eint.____ Ja, ja,

ja,   ja,   weißt nicht, wie   gut   ich   dir   bin._____
ja,   ja,   füh - le ich   ein - zig für   dich._____
ja,   ja,   weißt ja, wie   gut   ich   dir   bin._____
ja,   ja,   daß uns die   Lie - be ver - eint._____

SECTION 2: *ü, y*

The letter ü (sometimes also spelled *ue)* represents sounds that are variations of the sounds of *i.* The letter *y* follows the same rules for pronunciation as the letter ü.[7]

[yː] (lower-case y)

Long and closed [yː] is similar to long and closed [iː] but is pronounced with the lips rounded, as if for long and closed [uː].[8] Pronounce an extended [iːːːː] and, *without changing the position of the tongue or jaw,* slowly round the lips. Be aware that you are really pronouncing the sound [iː], but rounding as if for [uː]. For both [iː] and [yː], the sides of the tongue are against the upper back molars, and the tip of the tongue rests in the lower jaw against the bottom of the teeth. Only the rounding of the lips makes the distinction between the two sounds. Practice alternating [iː] and [yː] by slowly rounding and unrounding the lips while pronouncing [iːːːː].

The pronunciation of ü (and *y)* is regularly long and closed [yː] before a single consonant, as in *Güte ['gyːtə]* "goodness," *Lyrik* ['lyːrɪk] "lyrics," or before *h,* as in *fühlen* ['fyːlən] "feel."

---

[7]Except in some names and foreign words, e.g., *Fanny* ['fani], *York* [jɔrk].
[8]Since the lip position is the same as for [uː], the student may want to review that part of Section 6 below.

Exercise 6.12   Contrast the following pairs of words containing [iː] and [yː]:

1.	Stile	Stühle
2.	liegen	lügen
3.	sieden	Süden
4.	vier	für
5.	Triebe	trübe
6.	Miete	Mythe
7.	Riemen	rühmen
8.	Fliege	Flüge
9.	Biene	Bühne
10.	Tier	Tür

Exercise 6.13   Pronounce only the words with ü in Exercise 6.12.

Exceptions   There are a few words in which *ü* is long before two or more consonants.[9] Learn these:

1. before *st* in some words:

   Wüste ['vyːstə]   "desert"

   düster ['dyːstɐ]   "somber"

2. before *ch* in some words:

   Bücher ['byːçɐ]   "books"

   Tücher ['tyːçɐ]   "cloths"

   Psyche ['psyːçə]   "psyche"

Note: words with ß

In accordance with the spelling rules of 1996, a vowel followed by *ß* will be long. But, depending on the source and date of the text, the spelling of a word may not reflect this rule. The singer is advised to learn the following words with long *ü*, which may occasionally appear with *ss* instead of *ß:*

---

[9]Normally, ü is short before *st*, *ch*, *ss*, as expected.

büßen [ˈbyːsən]	"atone"
müßig [ˈmyːsɪç]	"leisurely"
süß [zyːs]	"sweet"
grüßen [ˈgʁyːsən]	"greet"
Füße [ˈfyːsə]	"feet"

[ʏ] (small capital Y)

Short and open [ʏ] is the same sound as short and open [ɪ] but is pronounced with the lips rounded, as if for short [ʊ].[10] Pronounce an extended [ɪːːːː] and, *without changing the position of the tongue or jaw*, slowly round the lips, but not as tightly as for [yː].

The position of the tongue is the same for both [ɪ] and [ʏ]. Only the rounding of the lips makes the distinction between the two sounds. Now practice alternating [ɪ] and [ʏ] by slowly rounding and unrounding the lips while pronouncing [ɪːːːː].

Be aware that [iː] and [yː] are closed sounds and that [ɪ] and [ʏ] are open sounds; that is, the jaw is slightly dropped for the latter.

The pronunciation of ü (and *y)* is regularly short and open [ʏ] before two or more consonants, as in *fünf* [fʏnf] "five," *idyllisch* [iˈdʏlɪʃ] "idyllic."

Exercise 6.14

Contrast [ɪ] and [ʏ] in the following pairs of words:

1. Kissen   küssen
2. Kiste   Küste
3. sticken   Stücken
4. missen   müssen
5. Gericht   Gerücht
6. ticken   Tücken
7. Minze   Münze
8. Kinde   künde

Exercise 6.15   Pronounce only the words with ü in Exercise 6.14.

---

[10]Since the lip position is the same as for [ʊ], the student may want to review that part of Section 6 below.

Exercise 6.16   Contrast long closed [yː] and short open [ʏ]:

1. Wüste	wüsste
2. fühle	fülle
3. rügte	rückte
4. Flüge	flügge
5. Hüte	Hütte
6. pflügte	pflückte
7. kühnste	Künste
8. büke	bücke

Exercise 6.17   Pronounce the following words, applying the rules for long or short monophthongs:

1. wütend, fühlen, Lyrik, Güte, Hülle
2. Wal'küre, dürfen, Hügel, flügge, Lüfte
3. mystisch, Hymne, Ana'lyse, Küste, Wüste, typisch
4. düster, rüsten, fünf, fürchten, für
5. müssen, büßen, süßen, wünschen, Münster
6. dürrer, Dürer, würde, i'dyllisch, grün, Gründe
7. Frühling, rhythmisch, blühen, Schüssel, flüstern

Exercise 6.18   Transcribe the above words into the IPA. Note: *w*=[v], prevocalic *s*=[z], *sch*=[ʃ]

Exercise 6.19   Read the following transcriptions aloud:

1. [bə'ryːmt, 'bryːdɐ, 'byːnə, 'flʏçtıç, 'bʏrgɐ]
2. ['drʏkən, 'dʏrə, 'kʏçə, 'gryːsən, 'hyːtən]
3. [fryː, 'fʏtɐn, 'flyːgəl, 'fʏlən, 'blyːtə]

Excerpts   1.

Durch tote Wüsten wandle hin,
Und grüne Schatten breiten sich,
Ob fürchterliche Schwüle dort
Ohn' Ende brüte, wonnevoll.

Through lifeless deserts wander forth
and green shade will spread itself—
though dreadful heat there
endlessly may brood—in bliss.

Wie bist du, meine Königin
Daumer/Brahms

   2.

Überm Garten durch die Lüfte
Hör' ich Wandervögel zieh'n,
Das bedeutet Frühlingsdüfte,
Unten fängt's schon an zu blüh'n.

Over the garden through the breezes
I hear passing birds;
that means spring fragrances—
below it's already beginning to bloom.

Frühlingsnacht
Eichendorff/Schumann

Song   Sing the following song, concentrating on the contrast between [yː] and [ʏ].

So sei gegrüßt viel tausendmal,
Holder, holder Frühling!
Willkommen hier in unserm Tal,
Holder, holder Frühling!
Holder Frühling überall
Grüßen wir dich froh mit Sang und Schall,
Mit Sang und Schall.

Du kommst und froh ist alle Welt,
Holder, holder Frühling!
Es freut sich Wiese, Wald und Feld,
Holder, holder Frühling!
Jubel tönt dir überall,
Dich begrüßet Lerch und Nachtigall,
Und Nachtigall.

So sei gegrüßt viel tausendmal,
Holder, holder Frühling!
O bleib recht lang in unserm Tal,
Holder, holder Frühling!
Kehr in alle Herzen ein,
Lass doch alle mit uns fröhlich sein,
Recht fröhlich sein.

So be greeted many thousand times,
lovely, lovely Spring!
Welcome here in our valley,
lovely, lovely Spring!
Lovely Spring, everywhere
we greet you joyously with song and noise,
with song and noise.

You arrive and joyous is all the world,
lovely, lovely Spring!
Happy are meadow, forest, and field,
lovely, lovely Spring!
Rejoicing rings out for you everywhere,
you are welcomed by lark and nightingale,
and nightingale.

So be greeted many thousand times,
lovely, lovely Spring!
Oh linger long in our valley,
lovely, lovely Spring!
Come into every heart,
and let all be joyful with us,
truly be joyful!

So sei gegrüßt viel tausendmal

SECTION 3: *e*

[eː] (lower-case E)

Long and closed [eː] is basically the first element of the English diphthong [eɪ], as in *gate* [geɪt]. In pronouncing [eɪ], note how the sides of the tongue slide inward along the molars and how the tip of the tongue and the jaw rise slightly.

In articulating the German sound [eː], as in *geht* [geːt] "goes," all movement of the tongue and jaw, and hence all trace of the English diphthongal element [ɪ], must be avoided. First practice pronouncing an extended [eːːːːː], allowing no movement of the tongue or jaw. Then practice pronouncing *geht*, exaggerating the length of the vowel [geːːːːː] and allowing the tip of the tongue to rise only when articulating the [t].

The pronunciation of *e* is regularly long and closed [eː]: (1) when it occurs before a single consonant, as in *beten* ['beːtən] "pray";[11] (2) when it occurs in a stressed syllable before *h*, as in *gehen* ['geːən] "go" (intervocalic *h* is not pronounced [see Chapter 13]); (3) when it occurs doubled, as in *Beet* [beːt] "flowerbed."

Exercise 6.20

Pronounce the following words containing [eː]:

1. Weh, stehlen, Sehnsucht, Ehre, Reh
2. Beet, Meer, Schnee, Klee, Fee
3. Weg, heben, legen, ewig, wer
4. den, dem, der, schwer, elend

Exceptions

In some words, *e* is long before two or more consonants. Memorize the following:

1. followed by *r* + consonant (only in these words, otherwise short):

erst [eːɐ̯st]	"first"
Erde ['eːɐ̯də]	"earth"

---

[11]In conversational German, the *e* is often pronounced open before *r* in short words like *er*, *wer*, *der*, and some singers tend to pronounce these words with [ɛ]. But because *e* is followed by a single consonant in such words, it should be pronounced closed: [eːɐ̯, veːɐ̯, deːɐ̯].

Herd [heːɐ̯t]	"hearth"
Schwert [ʃveːɐ̯t]	"sword"
wert [veːɐ̯t]	"worth"
Beschwerde [bəˈʃveːɐ̯də]	"complaint"
Pferd [pfeːɐ̯t]	"horse"
werden [ˈveɐ̯dən]	"become"
Erz [eːɐ̯ts][12]	"metal"

2. followed by other consonants:

stets [ʃteːts]	"always"
Krebs [kreːps]	"crab, cancer"
Dresden [ˈdreːsdən]	

[ɛ] (epsilon)

Short and open [ɛ] is approximately the same as the vowel sound in English *bet* but without any of the diphthongal elements typical of some accents in the United States.

Before two or more consonants *e* is usually short and open, as in *beste* [ˈbɛstə] "best," *Bett* [bɛt] "bed."

Exercise 6.21   Pronounce the following words containing [ɛ]:

1. Held, Bett, Recht, Nessel, helle

2. recken, gelb, denn, enden

3. Fest, beste, Heft, echt, fertig

Exceptions   In a few instances, *e* is short before a single consonant. Memorize the following:

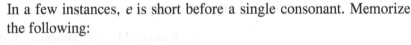

1. The short words:

es [ɛs]	"it"
des [dɛs]	"of the"
weg [vɛk]	"away"

---

[12]The word *Erz* "metal, ore" is pronounced with long [eː]; the syllable *Erz-* meaning "arch-" is pronounced with short [ɛ], e.g. *Erzengel* [ˈɛrtsˌʔɛŋəl] "archangel."

The particle *weg* [vɛk] "away" forms many compounds—for example *hin'weg, weggehen*—in which the vowel is always pronounced [ɛ]. This contrasts with the noun *Weg* [veːk] "way, path" and its compounds—e.g. *Wegweiser, Heimweg*—in which the vowel is always pronounced [eː]. Since the compounds of the noun *Weg* are also nouns, they will be capitalized and can generally be differentiated from the particle *weg* and its compounds, unless these should happen to appear at the beginning of a sentence.

2. The prefixes:

er- [ɛɐ̯]	as in *erkennen [ɛɐ̯'kenən]* "recognize"
ver [fɛɐ̯]	as in *verlieren* [fɛɐ̯'liːrən] "lose"
zer- [tsɛɐ̯]	as in *zerstören* [tsɛɐ̯'ʃtøːrən] "destroy"

These prefixes are pronounced with short [ɛ] whether they are followed by a vowel or a consonant.

Exercise 6.22

Differentiate between [eː] and [ɛ] in the following pairs:

1. Heer	Herr
2. den	denn
3. wen	wenn
4. Kehle	Kelle
5. legte	leckte
6. zehren	zerren
7. fehl	Fell
8. Beet	Bett

Exercise 6.23

Pronounce the following words, applying the rules for the pronunciation of long and short vowels:

1. See, Nebel, ewig, essen, hell, wehen
2. stehlen, Elend, bellen, bersten, ersten
3. stets, des, wer, Weh, flehen, Weg
4. geben, weg, es, Herd, Werk, Lerche, lernen
5. Herz, Erzengel, Erde, dem, 'Epik

Exercise 6.24   Transcribe the above words into the IPA. (Note: prevocalic *s*=[z]; *w*=[v]; initial *st*=[ʃt])

Unstressed e

Unstressed *e* is traditionally represented in reference works and text-books as [ə] (schwa). In actual practice, singers regularly use [ə] only for final e, as in *bitte* [ˈbɪtə] "please," and *e* in some unstressed middle syllables; and even in these cases the *e* tends to be more open than in spoken German.

Exercise 6.25   Pronounce the following words containing [ə]:

1. rechte, Stelle, lasse, kämme, hebe
2. lege, schwere, stehle, Ehre
3. Taugenichts, liebevoll, bessere, bittere

In all other unstressed syllables, but specifically in the prefixes *ge-* and *be-*, the adjective endings -*es*, -*en*, -*em*, and the verb endings -*en*, -*et*, -*est*, singers tend to front the vowel somewhat, achieving a quality more akin to [ɛ] than to [ə]. However, since the references use [ə] in transcribing these syllables, this text will also follow this practice. (See below for the prefixes *er-*, *ver-*, *zer-*, *emp-*, *ent-*.) The voice student is urged to listen carefully to established singers to determine how much and in what position [ɛ] can be fronted.

It is important to note that unstressed *e* is not long and closed if followed by *h* or any other single consonant. Thus *gehangen* "hung" and *gegeben* "given" would be transcribed [ɡəˈhaŋən, ɡəˈɡeːbən].

The Prefixes *er-*, *ver-*, *zer-*, *emp-*, *ent-*

In the prefixes *er-*, *ver-*, *zer-*, *emp-*, *ent-*, the *e* should always be pronounced and transcribed [ɛ], even though these syllables are almost always unstressed, as in *erfahren* [ɛɐ̯ˈfaːrən] "experience," *vergessen* [fɛɐ̯ˈɡɛsən] "forget."

Exercise 6.26   Pronounce the following words, paying special attention to the pronunciation of unstressed *e*:

1. gegeben, geehrt, begraben, beleben, geheimer
2. kühles, kühlen, kühlem
3. schweben, schwebest, schwebet

Exercise 6.27   Pronounce the following words, paying special attention to the pronunciation of unstressed *e*:

1. meine, meinen, meinem, Geliebte, Geliebten
2. stille, stilles, stillen, Garten, Sammetkleide
3. betend, werde, betreten, geteilt, betete

Exercise 6.28   Transcribe the words in Exercise 6.27 into the IPA. (Note: *ei*=[aɛ̯]; initial *st*=[ʃt]; prevocalic *s*=[z])

Excerpts   Read the following excerpts aloud, paying special attention to the pronunciation of unstressed *e*:

1.

Dem Schnee, dem Regen,	Facing the snow, the rain,
Dem Wind entgegen,	the wind,
Im Dampf der Klüfte,	in the mist of the ravines,
Durch Nebeldüfte.	through whiffs of fog.

Rastlose Liebe
Goethe/Schubert

2.

Wer trägt der Himmel unzählbare Sterne?	Who sustains the countless stars of the heavens?
Wer führt die Sonn' aus ihrem Zelt?	Who guides the sun from its canopy,
Sie kommt und leuchtet und lacht uns von ferne	to come and shine and beam at us from afar
Und läuft den Weg gleich als ein Held.	and stay its course just like a hero.
Kannst du der Wesen unzählbare Heere,	Can you observe the countless multitudes,
Den kleinsten Staub fühllos beschaun?	the smallest mote, unmoved?
Durch wen ist alles? O gib ihm die Ehre!	From whom comes all? Oh, give Him praise!
"Mir," ruft der Herr, "sollst du vertraun."	"In Me," calls the Lord, "shalt thou trust."

Die Ehre Gottes aus der Natur
Gellert/C.P.E. Bach

Song   Sing the following song, paying special attention to all *es*, accented and unaccented.

Guten Abend, gut' Nacht,	Good evening, good night,
Mit Rosen bedacht,	with roses covered,
Mit Näglein besteckt,	bedecked with carnations,
Schlüpf unter die Deck'.	slip under your blanket.
Morgen früh, wenn Gott will,	Tomorrow morning, if God will,
Wirst du wieder geweckt.	you'll be awakened again.
Guten Abend, gut' Nacht,	Good evening, good night,
Von Englein bewacht,	guarded by little angels—
Die zeigen im Traum	they'll show you in a dream
Dir Christkindleins Baum.	the little Christ Child's tree.
Schlaf nun selig und süß	Sleep now blissfully and sweetly,
Schau im Traum 's Paradies.	see Paradise in your dream.

Guten Abend, gut' Nacht

Deck'.   Mor - gen früh,   wenn Gott will,   wirst du   wie - der ge -
Baum.   Schlaf nun se - lig und süß, schau im Traum's Pa - ra -

weckt,___   mor - gen früh, wenn Gott will, wirst du wie - der ge - weckt.
dies,___   schlaf nun se - lig und süß, schau im Traum's Pa - ra - dies.

SECTION 4: ö

The letter ö (also sometimes spelled *oe*) represents sounds that are variations of the sounds of *e.*

[ø:] (slashed O, or O slash)

Long and closed [ø:] is similar to long and closed [e:] but is pronounced with the lips rounded, as for long and closed *o* [o:].[13] Pronounce an extended [e:::::] and, *without changing the position of the tongue or jaw*, slowly round the lips. Be aware that you are really pronouncing the sound [e:::::], but rounding as if for the sound [o:].

---

[13]Since the lip position is the same as for [o:], the student may want to review that part of Section 5 below.

Keep the sides of the tongue against the upper molars and the tip of the tongue against the base of the lower teeth; now, practice alternating [eː] and [øː] by slowly rounding and unrounding the lips while pronouncing [eːːːː].

The pronunciation of ö is regularly long and closed [øː] before a single consonant, as in *schön* [ʃøːn] "lovely," and before *h*, as in *fröhlich* ['frøːlɪç] "merry."

Exercise 6.29

Contrast [eː] and [øː] in the following pairs of words:

1. Meere   Möhre
2. Lehne   Löhne
3. lesen   lösen
4. Besen   bösen
5. verheeren   verhören
6. flehe   Flöhe
7. beten   böten
8. hebe   höbe
9. hehlen   Höhlen
10. sehne   Söhne

Exercise 6.30   Pronounce only the words with ö in Exercise 6.29 above.

Exceptions

There are a few words in which ö is pronounced long before two or more consonants.[14] Learn these:

1. before *st* in:

   trösten ['trøːstən]   "console"
   rösten ['røːstən]   "roast"

2. before *ch* in:

   höchst [høːçst]   "highest"

Note: words with ß

In accordance with the spelling rules of 1996, a vowel followed by *ß* will be long. But, depending on the source and date of the text, the

---

[14]Normally, ö is short before *st*, *ch*, *ss*, as expected.

spelling of a word may not reflect this rule. The singer is advised to learn the following words with long *ö*, which may occasionally appear with *ss* instead of *ß*.

Größe ['gʀøːsə]	"greatness"
größer-, größt- ['gʀøːsɐ, gʀøːst]	"greater, greatest"
Blöße ['bløːsə]	"bareness"
stößt [ʃtøːst]	"pushes"

[œ] (lower-case O-E ligature)

Short and open [œ] is the same as short and open [ɛ] but is pronounced with the lips rounded, as if for short and open [ɔ].[15] Pronounce an extended [ɛːːːː] and, *without changing the position of the tongue or jaw*, slowly round the lips, but not as much as for [øː]. Remember that [eː] and [øː] are both closed sounds and [ɛ] and [œ] are both open sounds.

Now practice alternating [ɛ] and [œ] by slowly rounding and unrounding the lips while pronouncing [ɛːːːː]. The pronunciation of ö is regularly short and open [œ] before two or more consonants, as in *könnte* ['kœntə] "could."

Exercise 6.31   Contrast [ɛ] and [œ] in the following pairs:

1. Mächte   möchte
2. stecke   Stöcke
3. helle   Hölle
4. Kellner   Kölner
5. fällig   völlig
6. fechte   föchte
7. Schwämme   schwömme
8. kernig   körnig

Exercise 6.32   Pronounce only the words with ö in Exercise 6.31 above.

---

[15]Since the lip position is the same as for [ɔ], the student may want to review that part of Section 6 below.

Exercise 6.33

Contrast [ø:] and [œ] in the following pairs:

1. Höhle   Hölle
2. gewöhnen   gewönnen
3. Söhne   sönne
4. Höker   Höcker
5. Schöße   schösse
6. blöken   Blöcken

Exercise 6.34

Pronounce the following words, applying the rules for long and short monophthongs:

1. versöhnen, böse, möchte, östlich, Getöse
2. öde, Töchter, plötzlich, töten, Schöpfer
3. nötig, Erlkönig, größte, schön, trösten
4. köstlich, höchstens, Dörflein, Blöße, schösse
5. höher, fröhlich, Löcher, völlig, könnte

Exercise 6.35

Transcribe the above examples into the IPA. (Note: v=[f]; prevocalic s=[z];)

Exercise 6.36

Read the following transcriptions aloud:

1. ['hø:ʀən, 'ʃtø:nən, 'lœʃən, 'tø:nə, gœnt]
2. [deːn, 'eːdəl, 'løːzən, dɛn, 'feːlɐ, 'lyːʀɪʃ]
3. ['hɛfstɪçstən, 'œfnən, 'løːvə, gəˈbeːt, veːɐ̯]
4. [iˈdeː, 'gœtɐ, 'kœʀpɐ, ɪnˈdeːm, hɪnˈvɛk]
5. ['plœtslɪç, mœnç, bəˈdaxt, 'flɛçtən, 'tøːtlɪç]

Excerpts   Read the following excerpts aloud, concentrating on the pronunciation of ö:

1.

Kömmt mir der Tag in die Gedanken,	(Whenever) that day comes into my thoughts,
Möcht' ich noch einmal rückwärts sehn,	I want to look back once again;
Möcht' ich zurücke wieder wanken,	I want to stumble back there
Vor ihrem Hause stille stehn.	(and) stand quietly before her house.

Die Winterreise
Müller/Schubert

2.

Will dich im Traum nicht stören,	(I) won't disturb you while dreaming
Wär' schad' um deine Ruh',	(it) would be a shame (to disturb) your rest,
Sollst meinen Tritt nicht hören—	(you) shall not hear my footsteps—
Sacht, sacht die Türe zu!	gently, gently, (I'll) close the door!

Die Winterreise
Müller/Schubert

Song   Sing the following song, concentrating on the pronunciation of ö.

Sah ein Knab' ein Röslein stehn,	A lad saw a little rose there,
Röslein auf der Heiden,	little rose upon the heath;
War so jung und morgenschön,	(it) was so young and lovely as morning,
Lief er schnell, es nah zu sehn,	he ran quickly to see it (up) close,
Sah's mit vielen Freuden.	(and he) saw it with great joy.
Röslein, Röslein, Röslein rot,	Little rose, little rose, little rose red,
Röslein auf der Heiden!	little rose on the heath!
Knabe sprach: "Ich breche dich,	(The) lad said: "I'll pluck you,
Röslein auf der Heiden!"	little rose on the heath!"
Röslein sprach: "Ich steche dich,	(The) little rose said: "I'll prick you
Dass du ewig denkst an mich,	(so) that you forever think of me,
Und ich will's nicht leiden."	and I will not suffer it."
Röslein, Röslein, Röslein rot,	Little rose, little rose, little rose red,
Röslein auf der Heiden!	little rose on the heath!
Und der wilde Knabe brach	And the crude lad plucked
's Röslein auf der Heiden.	the little rose on the heath.
Röslein wehrte sich und stach,	(The) little rose defended itself and pricked,
Half ihm doch kein Weh und Ach,	but no crying and wailing helped,
Musst' es eben leiden.	it just had to suffer.
Röslein, Röslein, Röslein rot,	Little rose, little rose, little red rose,
Röslein auf der Heiden!	little rose on the heath!

Heidenröslein

Hei - den, war so jung und mor - gen - schön, lief er schnell, es
Hei - den!" Rös - lein sprach: "Ich ste - che dich, daß du e - wig
Hei - den, Rös - lein wehr - te sich und stach, half ihm doch_ kein

nah zu sehn, sah's mit vie - len Freu - den. Rös - lein, Rös - lein
denkst an mich, und ich will's_ nicht lei - den." Rös - lein, Rös - lein
Weh und Ach, mußt' es e - ben lei - den. Rös - lein, Rös - lein

Rös - lein rot, Rös - lein auf der Hei - den!
Rös - lein rot, Rös - lein auf der Hei - den!
Rös - lein rot, Rös - lein auf der Hei - den!

SECTION 5: *o*

[oː] (lower-case O)

Long and closed [oː] is similar to the initial element in the English diphthong [oʊ], as in *lone* [loʊn]. In pronouncing [oʊ], note how the jaw and the tip of the tongue rise slightly for the second part of the diphthong.

In articulating the German sound [oː], as in *Lohn* [loːn] "wage," all movement of the tongue and jaw, and hence all trace of the English diphthongal element [ʊ], must be avoided. First, practice pronouncing an extended [oːːːːː], allowing no movement of the tongue or jaw. Then practice pronouncing *Lohn*, exaggerating the length of the vowel—[loːːːːːn]—and allowing the tip of the tongue to rise only when articulating the [n].

The pronunciation of *o* is regularly long and closed [oː]: (1) when it occurs before a single consonant, as in *schon* [ʃoːn] "already"; (2) when it occurs in a stressed syllable before *h*, as in *ohne* ['oːnə] "without"; (3) when it occurs doubled, as in *Boot* [boːt] "boat."

Exercise 6.37

Pronounce the following words containing long *o*:

1. ohne, Sohle, Lohn, froh, empfohlen, Kohle
2. Boot, Moos, Moor
3. Boden, holen, Monat, Vogel, Not, Los
4. Hof, Ton, rot, schon, Tor, Tod, vor

Exceptions

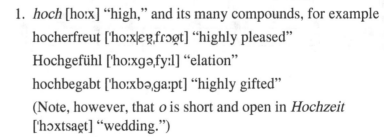

In a number of words, *o* is long and closed before two or more consonants.[16] Learn the following:

1. *hoch* [hoːx] "high," and its many compounds, for example
   hocherfreut ['hoːx|ɛɐ̯ˌfrɔøt] "highly pleased"
   Hochgefühl ['hoːxgəˌfyːl] "elation"
   hochbegabt ['hoːxbəˌgaːpt] "highly gifted"
   (Note, however, that *o* is short and open in *Hochzeit* ['hɔxtsaɛ̯t] "wedding.")

---

[16]Normally, *o* is short before *ch*, *st*, *ss*, as expected.

2. before *st* in these words:

Ostern ['oːstɐn]	"Easter"
Kloster ['kloːstɐ]	"cloister"
prost [proːst]	"to your health!"
Trost [troːst]	"solace"
getrost [gəˈtroːst]	"confident"

3. other words:

Mond [moːnt]	"moon"
Montag ['moːnˌtaːk]	"Monday"
Obst [oːpst]	"fruit"
Vogt [foːkt]	"warden, governor"

Note: words with ß

In accordance with the spelling rules of 1996, a vowel followed by *ß* will be long. But, depending on the source and date of the text, the spelling of a word may not reflect this rule. The singer is advised to learn the following words with long *o*, which may occasionally appear with *ss* instead of *ß*.

bloß [bloːs]	"bare, simply"
Schoß [ʃoːs]	"bosom, lap"
groß [groːs]	"large, great"
stoßen ['ʃtoːsən]	"push"

[ɔ] (open O)

Short and open [ɔ] is similar to the English sound represented by the same symbol, but it is usually much shorter and slightly more open. It is very much like the *o* sound in the British pronunciation of the word *hot*. The articulation of [ɔ] is similar to that for [o] but is further back.

Short [ɔ] occurs regularly before two or more consonants, as in *doch* [dɔx] "but."

Exercise 6.38   Pronounce the following words containing short *o*:

1. hoffen, kommen, wollen, fordern, Sporn, Rock

2. Sommer, Sonne, Wolke, voll, folgen, Schopf

3. stolz, Stock, Bock, dort, fort, Holz

4. Frosch, Groschen, doch, noch, Joch, Woche

Exceptions   In a few words, *o* is short and open before a single consonant. Learn the following:

ob [ɔp]   "whether"

von, vom [fɔn, fɔm]   "of, of the"

Exercise 6.39   Contrast [oː] and [ɔ]in the following pairs:

1. Gote   Gotte
2. wohne   Wonne
3. Tone   Tonne
4. bog   Bock
5. Wohle   Wolle
6. bohrte   Borte
7. Hofe   hoffe
8. Ofen   offen

Exercise 6.40   Pronounce the following words containing *o*, following the rules for long and short monophthongs:

1. Vogel, stolz, ohne, drohen, Tonne, mochte

2. Stoff, Mond, Dolch, Sonne, Sohn

3. hoch, Kloster, kosten, Posten, Ostern, Osten

4. Schoß, schoss, Schloss, großen, Ross, bloße

5. Hori'zont, Obst, ob, Ton, von, vom, Dom

6. Hochzeit, gestoßen, gegossen, Gold

7. em'por, 'Komik, da'von, froh'locken, Trost

Exercise 6.41   Transcribe the words in Exercise 6.40 above into the IPA. (Note: *v*=[f]; initial *st*=[ʃt]; *z*=[ts]; prevocalic *s*=[z]; *sch*=[ʃ]

Excerpts   Read the following excerpts aloud, paying careful attention to the pronunciation of *o*:

1.

Als müsste in dem Garten,	(It seems) as if in the garden,
Voll Rosen weiß und rot,	full of roses white and red,
Meine Liebste auf mich warten,	my dearest must be waiting for me,
Und ist doch lange tot.	and yet (she) is long dead.

Erinnerung
Eichendorff/Schumann

 2.

Alles nimmt sie, was nur hold,	It (night) takes everything, whatever (is) lovely,
Nimmt das Silber weg des Stroms,	takes the silver away from the stream,
Nimmt vom Kupferdach des Doms	takes from the copper roof of the cathedral
Weg das Gold.	the gold away.

Die Nacht
Gilm/Strauß

Song   Sing the following two songs, concentrating on the pronunciation of *o*.

Vor der Kaserne	Outside the barracks
Vor dem großen Tor	at the main gate
Stand eine Laterne	stood a lamppost,
Und steht sie noch davor,	and if it's still standing there
So woll'n wir da uns wiederseh'n,	then we'll see each other there again;
Bei der Laterne woll'n wir steh'n,	let's stand by that lamppost
Wie einst, Lili Marleen.	like (we did) then, Lili Marleen.
Unsre beiden Schatten	Our two shadows
Sah'n wie einer aus;	looked like one;
Dass wir so lieb uns hatten,	that we were in love,
Das sah man gleich daraus.	anyone could see that right away.
Und alle Leute soll'n es seh'n,	And everyone *should* see it
Wenn wir bei der Laterne steh'n,	when we stand by the lamppost
Wie einst, Lili Marleen.	like (we did) then, Lili Marleen.
Schon rief der Posten:	Already the sentry was calling:
"Sie blasen Zapfenstreich,	"They're playing taps (it's curfew)
es kann drei Tage kosten";	(and) it can cost (you) three days (if you're late)!"
"Kam'rad, ich komme gleich."	"Comrade, I'll come right away."
Da sagten wir "Auf Wiederseh'n,"	So we said goodbye;
Wie gerne wollt' ich mit dir geh'n,	how much I wanted to go with you,
Wie einst, Lili Marleen.	like then, Lili Marleen.
Deine Schritte kennt sie,	It (the lamppost) knows your footsteps
Deinen zieren Gang,	(and) your graceful gait;
Alle Abend brennt sie,	every night it's lit,
Doch mich vergaß sie lang.	but it forgot me long ago.
Und sollte mir ein Leid gescheh'n,	And (if) something should happen to me,
Wer wird bei der Laterne steh'n	who will stand by the lamp post
Mit dir, Lili Marleen?	with you, Lili Marleen?

Text: Hans Leip

Lili Marleen

Vor der Ka - ser - ne   vor dem gro - ßen Tor   stand 'ne La - ter - ne und
Uns-re bei - den Schat - ten   sah'n wie ei - ner aus; daß   wir so lieb uns hat - ten, das
Schon rief   der Po - sten:"sie   bla - sen Zap - fen - streich,   es kann drei Tage ko-sten;"Kam'-
Dei-ne Schritte   kennt sie,   dei - nen zie - ren Gang,   al - le A - bend brennt sie, doch

steht sie noch da - vor,   so woll'n wir da uns   wie - der - sehn, bei
sah man gleich dar - aus.   Und al - le Leu - te   soll'n es sehn, wenn
rad, ich kom - me gleich.   Da sag - ten wir "Auf   Wie - der - sehn," wie
mich ver - gaß   sie lang.   Und soll - te mir ein Leid   ge - schehn, wer

der   La - ter - ne   woll'n   wir   stehn,   wie   einst,   Li - li   Mar -
wir   bei   der   La - ter - ne   stehn,   wie   einst,   Li - li   Mar -
ger - ne   wollt'   ich   mit   dir   gehn,   wie   einst,   Li - li   Mar -
wird   bei   der   La - ter - ne   stehn,   mit   dir,   Li - li   Mar -

leen,   wie   einst,   Li - li   Mar - leen.
leen,   wie   einst,   Li - li   Mar - leen.
leen,   wie   einst,   Li - li   Mar - leen.
leen,   mit   dir,   Li - li   Mar - leen.

| O wie wohl ist mir am Abend | Oh, how fine I feel in the evening |
| Wenn zur Ruh die Glocken läuten | when the church bells call (us) to rest. |

Traditional Canon

O wie wohl ist mir am Abend

(Canon)

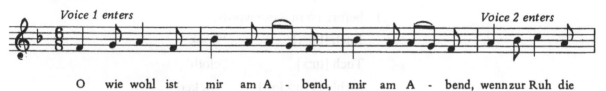

O   wie wohl ist   mir   am A - bend,   mir   am A -   bend, wennzur Ruh die

Glok - ken läu - ten, Glok - ken läu - ten, bim, bam,   bim, bam, bim, bam!

Song 6–6. O wie wohl ist mir am Abend

SECTION 6: *u*

[u:] (lower-case U)

German long and closed [u:] is similar to the English vowel in *moot*. For German [u:], as in *Mut* [mu:t], the lips are somewhat more protruded and somewhat more rounded than for the English sound. Long and closed [u:] occurs regularly before *h*, as in *Ruhe* ['ru:ə] "rest," or before a single consonant, as in *Flut* [flu:t] "flood."

Exercise 6.42   Pronounce the following words containing [u:]:

1. Kuh, Schuh, Huhn, Buhle, Uhr, Stuhl, Ruhe
2. rufen, gut, nun, schuf, Flug, Schule, Dur

Exceptions

In a number of words, *u* is long before two or more consonants.[17] Learn the following:

1. before *ch* in these words:

   Buch [buːx]   "book"

   Tuch [tuːx]   "cloth"

   ruchlos ['ruːxˌloːs]   "wicked"

   suchen ['zuːxən]   "seek"

   Fluch [fluːx]   "curse"

   Kuchen ['kuːxən]   "cake"

2. before *st* in these words:

   Schuster ['ʃuːstɐ]   "shoemaker"

   husten ['huːstən]   "cough"

3. also in

   Geburt [gə'buːɐ̯t]   "birth"

Note: words with ß

In accordance with the spelling rules of 1996, a vowel followed by *ß* will be long. But, depending on the source and date of the text, the spelling of a word may not reflect this rule. The singer is advised to learn the following words with long *u*, which may occasionally appear with *ss* instead of *ß*. (See also Chapter 10.)

   Buße ['buːsə]   "atonement"

   Fuß [fuːs]   "foot"

   Gruß [gruːs]   "greeting"

   Muße ['muːsə]   "leisure"

[ʊ] (upsilon, *also* horseshoe U)

German short and open [ʊ] is very similar to the vowel sound in English *puts*. It occurs regularly before two or more consonants, as in *Putz* [pʊts] "finery."

---

[17]Normally, *u* is short before *ch*, *st*, *ss*, as expected.

Exercise 6.43   Pronounce the following words containing [ʊ]:

1. Putz, Wunder, Kunst, Kupfer, Busch
2. Schutz, Luft, Druck, nutzen, bunt
3. Wunsch, gesund, Götterfunken, Puppe, dumm
4. muss, Fluss, Frucht, Flucht, wusste

Exceptions   There are a few words and syllables in which *u* is short before a single consonant. Learn the following:

um[18]	"around"
un- [ʊn]	prefix meaning *"un-,"* as in *unklar* [ˈʊnˌklaːɐ̯] "unclear"
zum [tsʊm]	"to the" (but note that, in accordance with the rules for length, *u* is long in *zu* [tsuː] "to," *zur* [tsuːɐ̯] "to the")
-us, e.g., *Jesus* [ˈjeːzʊs]	"Jesus"
Rum [ʀʊm]	"rum"

Exercise 6.44   Contrast [uː] and [ʊ] in the following pairs:

1. Mus   muss
2. Muhme   Mumme
3. schuft   Schuft
4. Ruhm   Rum
5. sucht   Sucht
6. spuken   spucken
7. Stuhle   Stulle
8. Buhle   Bulle
9. bucht   Bucht
10. flucht   Flucht
11. Flugs   flugs

---

[18]Also *um-, -um, -ium*, as in *Umlaut, Album, Oratorium* [ˈʊmˌlaɔ̯t, ˈalbʊm, oʀaˈtoːʀiʊm]

Exercise 6.45   Pronounce the following words containing *u*, applying the rules for long and short monophthongs: (Note that in some words the spelling does not reflect the modern rule for use of *ß* and *ss.*)

1. Flut, Mutter, Bube, du, rufen, Kunst, gute
2. Luft, Lust, Puls, Kurs, Kur, Kul'tur, hundert
3. Umsturz, Bucht, Buch, Kuß, Fluß, Fuß, Druck
4. Schuster, Muster, Demut, Fluch, fluchen
5. Blut, Armut, Bruch, Schuß, lustig, Brust, Jesus
6. Kutsche, genug, Geduld, Hochschule, Wollust
7. Wurzel, bewundern, Mund, Bursche, Genuß

Exercise 6.46   Transcribe the above words into the IPA.

Exercise 6.47   Read the following transcriptions aloud:

A. 1. ['buːlə, fluːk, zuːxt, frʊxt, hʊlt, jʊx'heː]
    2. [groːp, 'hoːnɪç, noːt, 'zɔndɐn, a'pɔstəl, zɔlç]
    3. [ɛɐ̯'faːrən, gə'nɔsən, gʊnst, fɛɐ̯'fluːxt, 'buːzən]

B. [zeː ɪç ziː am 'baxə 'zɪtsən

ven ziː 'fliːgənˌnetsə ʃtrɪkt

'oːdɐ 'zɔntaːks fyːɐ̯ diː 'fɛnstɐ

'frɪʃə 'viːzənˌbluːmən pflʏkt

zeː ɪç ziː tsʊm 'gartən 'vandəln

mɪt deːm 'kœrpçən ɪn deːɐ̯ hant

naːx deːn 'eːɐ̯stən 'beːrən 'ʃpeːən

an deːɐ̯ 'gryːnən 'dɔrnənˌvant]

Excerpts   Read the following excerpts aloud, paying special attention to the pronunciation of *u:*

1.

Herzeleid und viel Verdruss,	Heartbreak and much trouble,
Eine Schul' und enge Mauern,	a school and confining walls,
Carreaukönig, der bedauern	(the) King of Diamonds, who must pity
Und zuletzt mich trösten muss.	and, in the end, comfort me.
Ein Geschenk auf art'ge Weise,	A gift (given) with propriety,
Er entführt mich—eine Reise—	he abducts me—a journey—
Geld und Lust im Überfluss!	money and pleasure in abundance!

Die Kartenlegerin
Chamisso/R. Schumann

2.

Und du singst, was ich gesungen,	And you sing what I (have) sung,
Was mir aus der vollen Brust	which from my full heart,
Ohne Kunstgepräng' erklungen,	without artifice, (has) sprung,
Nur der Sehnsucht sich bewusst.	conscious only of longing.

An die ferne Geliebte
Jeitteles/Beethoven

Recording   Practice reading the lyrics of the following song. Then record them without pausing.

Song   Sing the following song, concentrating on the pronunciation of *u*.

Ich weiß nicht, was soll es bedeuten,
Daß ich so traurig bin;
Ein Märchen aus alten Zeiten,
Das kommt mir nicht aus dem Sinn.

Die Luft ist kühl und es dunkelt
Und ruhig fließt der Rhein;
Der Gipfel des Berges funkelt
im Abendsonnenschein.

Die schönste Jungfrau sitzet
dort oben wunderbar;
Ihr gold'nes Geschmeide blitzet,
Sie kämmt ihr goldenes Haar.

Sie kämmt es mit goldenem Kamme
Und singt ein Lied dabei,
Das hat eine wundersame,
gewalt'ge Melodei.

Den Schiffer im kleinen Schiffe
ergreift es mit wildem Weh;
Er schaut nicht die Felsenriffe,
er schaut nur hinauf in die Höh'.

Ich glaube, die Wellen verschlingen
am Ende Schiffer und Kahn,
Und das hat mit ihrem Singen
die Lorelei getan.

I don't know what it might mean
that I am so sad,
a tale from olden times
that I can't get out of my mind.

The air is cool and it's growing dark,
and peacefully flows the Rhine;
the top of the mountain gleams
in the evening sunlight.

The loveliest maiden sits
wondrously up above;
her golden jewels sparkle,
she combs her golden hair.

She combs it with (a) golden comb
while singing a song
that has a wondrous,
powerful melody.

The boatman in the little boat
is seized with mad pangs;
he sees not the rocky reefs,
he just gazes up above.

I believe the waves engulf
boatman and boat in the end,
and that, with her singing,
the Lorelei has done.

Text: Heine

Die Lorelei

Ich weiß nicht, was soll es be - deu - ten, daß ich so trau - rig
Die schön - ste Jung - frau sit - zet dort o - ben wun - der -
Den Schif - fer im klei - nen Schif - fe er - greift es mit wil - dem

bin;____ ein Mär - chen aus al - ten Zei - ten, das
bar;____ ihr gold' - nes Ge - schmei - de blit - zet, sie
Weh;____ er schaut nicht die Fel - sen - rif - fe, er

kommt mir nicht aus dem Sinn.____ Die Luft ____ ist kühl und es
kämmt ihr gol - de - nes Haar.____ Sie kämmt es mit gol - de - nem
schaut nur hin - auf in die Höh'.____ Ich glau - be die Wel - len ver -

dun - kelt und ru - hig fließt ___ der Rhein; ___ der
Kam - me und singt ein Lied ___ da - bei, ___ das
schlin - gen am En - de Schif - fer und Kahn ___ und

Gip - fel des Ber - ges fun - kelt im A - bend - son - nen - schein. ___
hat ei - ne wun - der - sa - me ge - walt' - ge Me - lo - dei. ___
das hat mit ih - rem Sin - gen die Lo - re - lei ___ ge - tan. ___

Word Structure and Stress

SECTION 1: STRUCTURAL ELEMENTS

There are certain problems of pronunciation that can be resolved only through a knowledge of German word structure. These problems require identification of four main types of structural elements: (A) prefixes; (B) suffixes; (C) parts of compound words; (D) inflectional endings. Perhaps surprisingly, the rules for syllable division in simple words do not always provide significant information in determining pronunciation.[1]

---

[1]Although the rules for syllable division in simple words do not provide significant help in determining pronunciation, they are outlined below for the singer's information since every musical score contains words that are divided into syllables to be sung on different notes.

    1. Division falls before a single consonant: *ge-ben, Frie-den*. Because *ch, sch, ß, ph,* and *th* represent single sounds, the syllable division falls before them: *Be-cher, lö-schen, Stra-ße, Te-le-phon, A-po-the-ke.*

    2. Division falls before the final consonant of a cluster: *kämp-fen, hol-der, sen-den.* The combination *ck* is written *k-k* when divided: *blicken = blik-ken.*

    3. Although in simple words double consonants represent single sounds, they are separated in syllable division: *ret-ten, Was-ser, hel-le.*

    4. The combination *st,* although it represents two sounds, is never separated in simple words: *be-ste, Mei-ster.*

A. Prefixes

The following is a list of common German prefixes. Since these prefixes can have a significant effect on the pronunciation of a word, they should be learned for recognition.

You will recall that several prefixes do not conform to the rules of pronunciation; transcriptions of these prefixes are provided. The pronunciation of each prefix is constant regardless of what follows it since a prefix always constitutes a separate structural element in a word.

Stressed

Except for *ur-*, these are *separable* prefixes—that is, they may appear separated from the stem in certain verb forms. They will generally be stressed.[2]

ab- [ap]	abreisen	[ˈapˌraeɡzən]	"depart"
an- [an]	ankommen	[ˈanˌkɔmən]	"arrive"
auf-	aufsehen	[ˈaɔfˌzeːən]	"look up"
aus-	ausruhen	[ˈaɔsˌruːən]	"rest"
bei-	Beifall	[ˈbaeˌfal]	"applause"
dar-	darstellen	[ˈdaːɐˌʃtɛlən]	"represent"
ein-	einsingen	[ˈaenˌzɪŋən]	"practice singing"
fort-	fortlaufen	[ˈfɔrtˌlaɔfən]	"run away"
her- [heːɐ, hɛɐ][3]	herkommen	[ˈheːɐˌkɔmən]	"come here"
hin- [hɪn]	hingehen	[ˈhɪnˌgeːən]	"go there"
mit- [mɪt]	mitgehen	[ˈmɪtˌgeːən]	"go along"
nach- [naːx]	nacheilen	[ˈnaːxˌaeɡlən]	"hurry after"
ur-	Urwald	[ˈuːɐˌvalt]	"primeval forest"
vor-	Vorsicht	[ˈfoːɐˌzɪçt]	"caution"
weg- [vɛk][4]	weggehen	[ˈvɛkˌgeːən]	"go away"
zu-	zueilen	[ˈtsuːˌaeɡlən]	"hurry to"

---

[2]In some cases, especially when a prefix is combined with another prefix, the stress may not fall on the first syllable: *zuvor* [tsuˈfoːɐ], *vorbei* [foɐˈbae]. See also note on *her-, hin-, dar-, vor-* in Section IV.A.

[3]When *her-* is stressed, as in *herkommen* [ˈheːɐˌkɔmən] "come here" or when it stands alone, it is pronounced [heːɐ]; when it is unstressed, as in *hervor* [hɛɐˈfoːɐ] "forth," it is pronounced [hɛɐ]. Note, however, that *e* is short in *Herzog* [ˈhɛrtsoːk] "duke."

[4]The *e* in the prefix *weg-* is short, but recall that in the noun *Weg* [veːk] "way" and its compounds the *e* is long.

Unstressed

The following are *inseparable* prefixes, which will remain attached to the stem. In words with these prefixes, the stress will fall on the following element. Since there are many words with these prefixes in song literature, the singer should memorize these prefixes.

be- [bə]	beglücken	[bə'glʏkən]	"make happy"
ent-[5]	entlaufen	[ɛnt'laɔfən]	"run away"
er- [ɛɐ̯]	erfüllen	[ɛɐ̯'fʏlən]	"fulfill"
ge- [gə]	gesehen	[gə'zeːən]	"seen"
ver- [fɛɐ̯]	vergolden	[fɛɐ̯'gɔldən]	"gild"
zer- [tsɛɐ̯]	zerreißen	[tsɛɐ̯'raɛsən]	"rip up"

Stressed–Unstressed[6]

In words containing these prefixes, the stress falls on the prefix in some words and on the stem in others. Nouns containing these prefixes (recall that nouns are capitalized) will, in general, have the stress on the prefix. For the exercises in this book, assume that words containing these prefixes will have the stress on the prefix, unless otherwise indicated.

da-	dafür	[da'fyːɐ̯, 'daːfyɐ̯]	"for it"
durch-	durchspielen	['dʊrçʃpiːlən]	"play through"
miss-	Misstrauen	['mɪsˌtraɔən]	"mistrust" (noun)
	misstrauen	[mɪs'traɔən]	"mistrust" (verb)
über-	Überfluss	['yːbɐˌflʊs]	"abundance"
um- [ʊm]	Umweg	['ʊmˌveːk]	"detour"
un- [ʊn]	unglücklich	['ʊnglʏklɪç]	"unhappy"
unter-	unterirdisch	['ʊntɐˌɪrdɪʃ]	"subterranean"
wider-	Widerhall	['viːdɐˌhal]	"echo"
	widersprechen	[viːdɐ'ʃprɛçən]	"contradict"

---

[5]The variant *emp-* appears in a few words, e.g. *empfangen* [ɛm'pfaŋən] "receive," *empfehlen* [ɛm'pfeːlən] "recommend," *empfinden* [ɛm'pfɪndən] "feel, sense."

[6]Unfortunately, there is no simple rule to determine the placement of stress in words containing these prefixes. Consult Siebs (pp. 117–129) for lists indicating the stress in such words.

B. Suffixes

The most common German suffixes are:

-bar	trinkbar	['trɪŋkˌbaːɐ̯]	"drinkable"
-chen	Männchen	['mɛnˌçən]	"little man"
-haft	mannhaft	['manˌhaft]	"manly"
-heit	Kindheit	['kɪntˌhaɛ̯t]	"childhood"
-keit	Göttlichkeit	['gœtlɪçˌkaɛ̯t]	"godliness"
-lein	Männlein	['mɛnˌlaɛ̯n]	"little man"
-lich	freundlich	['frɔɡ̊ntˌlɪç]	"friendly"
-los	herzlos	['hɛrtsˌloːs]	"heartless"
-nis [nɪs]	Finsternis	['fɪnstɐˌnɪs]	"darkness"
-sal	Trübsal	['tryːpˌzaːl]	"sorrow"
-sam	wachsam	['vaxˌzaːm]	"wakeful"
-schaft	Landschaft	['lantˌʃaft]	"landscape"
-tum	Reichtum	['raɛ̯çˌtuːm]	"wealth"

C. Compound Words

German is well known for its many compound words, such as *Waldeinsamkeit* and *Meistersinger.* In many instances, the singer must be able to break the words into their component elements in order to pronounce them correctly. Some words are simply put together, such as *Meistersinger.* Others are joined with a connective element. It is helpful to be able to recognize the four common connective elements: (1) *e,* as in *Hundehütte;* (2) *(e)n,* as in *Rosenblatt;* (3) *er,* as in *Kindergarten;* (4) *(e)s,* as in *Liebestraum.* Fortunately, it is usually apparent how compounds should be divided; however, for some words, the singer must have some knowledge of German in order to decide pronunciation questions such as unvoicing or division of consonant clusters.

D. Inflectional Endings

Frequently, the singer needs to have a knowledge of inflection, especially verb inflection, in order to resolve questions concerning pronunciation.

Below are parts of a model verb, *legen,* "to lay or put," which will be used to illustrate certain pronunciation problems.

Present tense:

ich lege	"I lay"	wir legen	"we lay"
du legst	"you (singular) lay"	ihr legt	"you (plural) lay"
er, sie, es legt	"he, she, it lays"	sie legen	"they lay"

Past tense:

ich legte	"I laid," etc.	wir legten
du legtest		ihr legtet
er, sie, es legte		sie legten

Past participle:

gelegt   "laid," as in "I have *laid*"

Another ending that the student should be able to recognize is the genitive singular *-s* of nouns, as in *Betrugs,* genitive of *Betrug* "betrayal."

SECTION 2: STRESS[7]

Primary Stress

In Chapter 4 we stated that in words of Germanic origin, the main, or primary, stress generally falls on the first syllable; in this chapter we discuss words with certain prefixes, in which the primary stress falls on the following syllable.

Secondary Stress

Siebs points out (p. 115) that, in addition to stressed syllables and unstressed syllables, as in *Kinder* ['kɪndɐ], many German words also contain syllables that exhibit a secondary stress, not quite as strong as the primary stress, as in *Kindergarten* ['kɪndɐˌgartən]; this stress

---

[7]See Section 5 below for stress in loan words.

is indicated with a short vertical line below and to the left of the element. This also affects certain suffixes; Siebs gives the following examples: *'Frei₁heit, 'Siche₁rung, 'Köni₁gin, 'heil₁sam, 'fabel₁haft, 'feier₁lich, 'furcht₁bar.* Although the symbol does not appear extensively in transcriptions in Siebs or Duden, we will often include it in examples in this text, as it can help keep the student aware of the existence of the secondary stress, as well as indicate where one element ends and another begins.

SECTION 3: PRONUNCIATION PROBLEMS

There are four main types of pronunciation problems that may require a knowledge of the structural elements: (I) vowel length; (II) unvoicing; (III) consonant clusters; (IV) glottal separation.

I. Vowel Length

In Chapter 6, it was pointed out that a vowel followed by a single consonant is usually long.[8] In compounds and inflected forms, vowels that are *apparently* followed by two or more consonants are often long. The words must be broken down into structural elements in order to determine whether the vowel is in fact followed by a single consonant or more than one consonant.

A. Prefixes

In general, the pronunciation of a prefix remains the same, regardless of what follows it. Thus the vowel in *vor-* is long whether the prefix is followed by a vowel or a consonant: *Voreltern* ['foːɐ̯|ɛltɐn] "ancestors," *Vorvater* ['foːɐ̯ˌfaːtɐ] "forefather."

A number of prefixes are pronounced with a short vowel even though they end with a single consonant (see list under "Prefixes," above and Chapter 6); this pronunciation is not affected by what follows the prefix. Thus the vowel in *mit* is short whether the prefix is followed by a vowel or a consonant: *mitessen* ['mɪt|ɛsən] "dine with," *mitgehen* ['mɪtˌgeːən] "go along."

---

[8]Recall that the vowels treated in Chapter 6 are closed as well as long when they occur before a single consonant.

B. Suffixes

If the element before a suffix ends in a single consonant, as in *Röslein* "little rose," then the vowel is long: ['rø:s‚laɛn].

Exercise 7.1

Pronounce the following words:

1. lesbar, Blümchen, boshaft, Bosheit, Röslein
2. tödlich, tonlos, Verlöbnis, Trübsal, strebsam, Botschaft

C. Compounds

If a compound divides so that a vowel is followed by a single consonant as in *Betbuch* "prayer book," then the vowel is long: ['be:t‚bu:x].

Exercise 7.2

Pronounce the following words:

1. Bluttat, dem'selben, Flughafen, Lebtag
2. Lobgesang, Blutgeld, losgeben, für'wahr, Hofleute
3. jedweder, Rotkäppchen, totschlagen, Fluggast
4. Gutteil, Betstunde, Brotherr, Wegweiser, Tonkunst

D. Inflection

If a verb has a long vowel in the infinitive, then that vowel will normally be pronounced long regardless of inflectional endings.

Infinitive:

legen   ['le:gən] "to lay"

Present tense:

du legst   [le:kst] "you lay"

er legt   [le:kt] "he lays"

etc.

Past tense:

ich legte   ['le:ktə] "I laid"

etc.

Past participle:

gelegt   [gə'le:kt] "(have) laid"

Likewise, if a noun has a long vowel, the presence of an inflectional ending will not affect the quality of the vowel.

Nominative:

Betrug   [bə'tru:k] "betrayal"

Genitive:

Betrugs   [bə'tɾuːks] "(of) betrayal"

Words ending in *-el, -en,* and *-er* often lose the *e* when adding inflectional endings or suffixes. (Use the name *Eleanor* to remember these syllables.) This does not affect the length of a preceding vowel (see also next section, "Unvoicing").

edel ['eːdəl] "noble"   edle ['eːdlə] "noble"

Ekel ['eːkəl] "disgust"   eklig ['eːklɪç] "disgusting"

wider ['viːdɐ] "against"   widrig ['viːdɾɪç] "adverse"

Exercise 7.3

Pronounce the following words containing inflectional endings:

1. lebst, bewegt, verlobt, klebt, Bahnhofs

2. verflucht, beschwört, beschert, gegrüßt, getönt

3. betont, Berufs, tobst, gelöst

4. grünst, büßte, hegte, lebtest

II. Unvoicing

The consonants *b, d, g,* and *s*[9] are pronounced as their voiceless equivalents [p, t, k, s][10] when they occur: (1) at the end of a word, as in *Bad* [baːt] "bath"; (2) before a consonant, as in *Magd* [maːkt] "maid"; and (3) at the end of an element, as in *Abendessen* ['aːbənt‚ɛsən] "supper."

Exercise 7.4

Pronounce the following:

1. Tag	5. Vogt
2. Bad	6. Abt
3. Mond	7. beredt
4. leb'	

---

[9]The consonant *v* is also affected to some extent by these rules (see Chapter 16); *w* is only rarely affected.

[10]As one might expect, there is a slight difference in articulation, e.g. in *Bad* vs. *bat,* but the difference is subtle and will not be discussed in this book.

A. Prefixes

The only important prefix ending in one of these consonants is *ab-*. It is always pronounced [ap], as in *abändern* ['ap‚ɛndɐn] "transform," *ablegen* ['ap‚leːgən] "take off." The singer is cautioned about words such as *aber* ['aːbɐ] "but" and *Abend* ['aːbənt] "evening," in which *ab* is not a prefix.

Exercise 7.5 Pronounce the following:

1. ablegen
2. abspielen
3. abgeneigt
4. aberkennen
5. Aberglaube
6. Abendmahl

B. Suffixes

A number of suffixes begin with consonants, and *b, d, g,* and *s* will be unvoiced before them, as in *freundlich, endlos, Wildnis, strebsam,* and *lesbar.*[11] However, this does not really represent a special case of the general rule, which states simply that *b, d, g,* and *s* are unvoiced before consonants.

When *b, d, g,* and *s* occur before *l, n,* and *r* in inflected forms and derivatives of words ending in *-el, -en,* or *-er,* they are *not* usually unvoiced. (Remember *Eleanor!*) It will not always be easy for the singer with only a passing knowledge of German to recognize such forms. A number of examples are listed in Exercise 7.6 below to provide some familiarity with the type. Recall from the previous section ("Vowel Length") that long vowels remain long in inflected forms and derivatives such as *edle* ['eːdlə], *ebne* ['eːbnə].

Exercise 7.6 Pronounce the following words, paying special attention to *b, d, g, s:*

1. siedle (< siedeln) "settle"
2. Siedlung (< siedeln) "settlement"
3. edle (< edel) "noble"
4. Adlige (< Adel) "aristocrat(s)"
5. Adler (< Adel) "eagle"
6. ebne (< eben) "smooth"
7. übler (< übel) "foul"

[11]Some singers prefer to voice these consonants before *-lich* and certain other suffixes: ['liːb‚lɪç]. (Siebs also reflects this pronunciation.)

8. goldne (< golden) "golden"

9. handle (< handeln) "act"

10. eigner (< eigen) "(one's) own"

11. andre (< ander) "other"

12. seidnes (< seiden) "silken"

13. Wandrer (< wandern) "wanderer"

14. Wagner (< Wagen) "cartwright"

15. Wandlung (< wandeln) "transformation"

16. Bogner (< Bogen) "bow-maker"

17. regnet (< Regen) "(it) rains"

18. irdne (< irden) "earthen"

19. Redner (< reden) "orator"

20. Ordnung (< older *ordenung)* "order"

21. unsre (< unser) "our"

22. heisrem (< heiser) "hoarse"

23. Gegner (< gegen) "opponent"

24. Lügner (< lügen) "liar"

C. Compounds

If an element in a compound ends in *b, d, g,* or *s* and is followed by an element beginning with a consonant, as in *Mondschein* "moonlight" or *Diebstahl* "theft," the final *b, d, g,* or *s* in that element is of course unvoiced: ['moːntʃaɛn, 'diːpʃtaːl], since *b, d, g, s* are unvoiced before any consonant.

If, however, the second element begins with a vowel, the singer must be able to break down the word in order to know that the consonant is at the end of the first element and unvoiced, rather than at the beginning of the second element and voiced. In *Lesart* ['leːs|aːɐ̯t] "version" and *Blasinstrument* ['blaːs|ɪnstru̩ˌment] "wind instrument," for example, it is important to recognize that *s* belongs to the first element and is pronounced [s]; if it belonged to the second element, it would be pronounced [z].

Exercise 7.7   Pronounce the following:

1. Lobgesang
2. Abendsonne
3. berg'ab
4. berg'auf
5. endgültig

6. Argwohn
7. Abendessen
8. bandartig
9. Bergsteiger
10. Bildhauer

Inflectional Endings

If a voiced consonant appears before an ending beginning with a consonant, then it of course becomes unvoiced: *legst* [leːkst], *legt* [leːkt], *gelegt* [gəˈleːkt], *Betrugs* [bəˈtruːks]. It will not be unvoiced before an ending beginning with a vowel: *legest* [ˈleːgəst].

It frequently happens that an inflectional ending is dropped in a song text, reflecting common spoken practice: *hab' ich* "have I" instead of *habe ich*. Strictly speaking, the final consonant in such a case should become unvoiced [haːp ɪç], and indeed many singers use this articulation. However, many singers prefer to maintain the voicing as if the *e* ending were still there: [ˈhaːb ɪç]. Unfortunately, scores do not consistently use the apostrophe to indicate that an ending has been dropped.

III. Consonant Clusters

Certain combinations of consonants have a particular pronunciation when they appear together in a simple word. If, however, the same consonants appear together, but belong to different elements in a word, they must be pronounced not as a unit but as parts of the separate elements.

For example, *sch* is pronounced [ʃ] in a simple word such as *löschen* [ˈlœʃən] "extinguish." If, however, *s* and *ch* come together as parts of two different elements, as they do in *Röschen* "little rose," then this must be reflected in the pronunciation: [ˈrøːsˌçən].

In simple words, double consonants are usually pronounced the same as single consonants, for example, in *Betten* [ˈbɛtən] "beds." If, on the other hand, the double consonant represents parts of two elements, as in *Bettag* "day of prayer," the release of the *t* is delayed: [ˈbɛtˌtaːk]. Some sources indicate this phenomenon with a tie bar: [ˈbɛt͜taːk].

The following consonant clusters occur frequently in German:

bl	br
	dr
fl	fr
gl	gr
kl	kr
pl	pr
	tr

schl   schr   schm   schn

If one of the above clusters occurs in one element, it is called a *blend* and is pronounced as a single unit. If, however, part of such a combination belongs to one element and part to another, each part of the combination is pronounced with its respective element. Contrast for example *zu'gleich (zu + gleich)* "together," pronounced [tsu'glaɛç], and *Zugluft (Zug + Luft)* "draft" (of air), pronounced ['tsuːkˌlʊft]. The difference is in some instances more striking in singing than in speaking. A combination such as *bl, kr, fl* will be launched on one note if it belongs to one element; if, however, the combination is composed of parts of two elements, the first part will be sung on one note, the second on the next.

A. Prefixes

Since a number of prefixes end in consonants, a variety of consonant combinations occurs in words containing prefixes. The prefix always constitutes a separate element, and its final consonant should not be tied over to the next element.

Exercise 7.8

1. Pronounce the following words.

2. Indicate whether a consonant cluster is divided by placing a slash, e.g. *zu/gleich, Zug/luft.*

3. Transcribe into the IPA.

   1. abrennen, abbrennen, angehen, Vorrat, Verrat

   2. entrüstet, unnötig, fortrennen, herritt, Hinnahme

B. Suffixes

Because a number of suffixes begin with consonants, various consonant combinations occur in words containing suffixes. The suffix always constitutes a separate element, and a final consonant in the preceding element should not be tied over to an initial consonant in the suffix.

Exercise 7.9

1. Pronounce the following words.

2. Indicate whether a consonant cluster is divided by placing a slash, e.g. *lieb/lich ['liːpˌlɪç].*[12]

3. Transcribe into the IPA. (Note: prevocalic *s*=[z], *sch*=[ʃ], *ei*=[ae̯])

    1. unglaublich
    2. endlich
    3. sorglos
    4. Derbheit
    5. verschiebbar

C. Compounds

Also in compounds, problem clusters may be formed at the junction of two elements. Here too, each element is pronounced separately, and consonant sounds are not blended across the boundary. Observe the separation of consonants in the compound *Zug/luft* ['tsuːkˌlʊft] "draft" (literally, "draft air").

The final consonant of the connecting elements *(e)s, er, (e)n* will always be separated from following consonants, as in *Todes/tag* ['toːdəsˌtaːk] "day of death."

Exercise 7.10

1. Pronounce the following words.

2. Indicate whether a consonant cluster is divided by placing a slash, e.g. *Todes/tag.*

3. Transcribe into the IPA.
    1. arglistig, Arbeitstisch, Betstunde, Dankrede
    2. Donnerstag, Festrede, huldreich, Bergland

D. Inflection

Problem consonant clusters are not generally formed by the addition of inflectional endings.

---

[12]Especially with the suffixes *-lich* and *-los*, voicing of a preceding consonant is often heard: ['liːblɪç].

It should be clear from the foregoing section on consonant clusters that some knowledge of German is necessary in order to determine how to divide some problem clusters. The novice cannot be expected to know how to divide *Zugluft* or *zugleich*. Or consider the unusual form *erblich*. As a verb meaning "grew pale," it is divided into the prefix *er-* and the root *blich* and is pronounced [ɛɐ̯'blɪç]. As an adjective meaning "hereditary," it is divided into the root *erb-* and the suffix *-lich* and is pronounced ['ɛrpˌlɪç]. It is clear from these examples that it is important to learn to recognize the prefixes, suffixes, and inflectional endings. Then, as consonant clusters are treated in greater detail in the following sections, it should be easier for the singer to develop some skill in determining how to divide them.

IV. Glottal Separation [|]

In traditional linguistics, the glottal stop is the brief stoppage of air before articulating a following vowel and is indicated by the symbol [ʔ]. It can prevent *an aim* [ən ʔeɪm] from sounding like *a name* [ə neɪm].

In German, every word beginning with a vowel is preceded by a glottal stop. In singing, however, it is generally recommended not to use a complete glottal stop with every word beginning with a vowel, rather a softer closure of the glottis.

Exercise 7.11

Practice separating with a soft closure the words beginning with a vowel in the following phrases:

1. die alte Amme
2. der erste Akt
3. ein altes Erbe

Many texts and references use the symbol [ʔ] for glottal stop. We will use the symbol [|], which also appears in Siebs and Duden. There it is stressed that the symbol is used not so much to indicate a glottal stop *per se* as a break in the legato flow within a word. Thus the symbol [|] appears in Siebs and Duden primarily within a word rather than at the beginning. Although many singers feel that it is important to begin most words starting with a vowel with a glottal stop, we will focus our attention on its use within words, where it can serve to separate elements.[13]

---

[13]In transcriptions of longer excerpts, we will also use the symbol initially.

A. Prefixes

As we have pointed out, any prefix constitutes a separate element and should be pronounced as a unit. If the prefix is followed by a vowel, the vowel will usually be preceded by a glottal separation, as in *erinnern* [ɛɐ̯|ˈɪnɐn] "remember," *beachten* [bəˈ|axtən] "take heed."

The prefixes *her-, hin-, dar-,* and *vor-* represent a special case. When they are combined with another prefix beginning with a vowel, there is no glottal separation and the final consonant is drawn to the following syllable with the stress falling on the second syllable, as in *heran* [hɛˈran] "hither," *hinan* [hɪˈnan] "upward," *daran* [daˈran] "to it," and *voran* [foˈran] "forward."

When *her-, hin-, dar-,* and *vor-* appear before an element other than another prefix, they are pronounced as a unit and followed by a glottal separation if the element begins with a vowel, as in *Vorahnung* [ˈfoɐ̯|aːnʊŋ] "premonition." As a general rule, of these four prefixes only *vor-* will appear before an element that begins with a vowel but is not a prefix.

Exercise 7.12

Pronounce the following words, using a glottal separation where appropriate. Review the rules regarding stress at the beginning of this chapter. Some words may have more than one stress option; unless the word begins with a prefix that is unstressed in accordance with the rules, assume initial stress unless otherwise indicated.

1. abändern, beobachten, aneignen, auferstehen, fort'an
2. ausatmen, einatmen, entarten, erinnern, über'antwortet
3. geahnt, geehrt, vereint, Mitarbeiter, unterirdisch
4. nachahmen, über'all, vorangehen, vorauseilen, Vorort
5. daraus, miss'achten, herannahen, uralt, un'endlich
6. beiordnen, beirren, durch'irren, wegessen, umändern
7. hineingehen, zu'erst, forteilen, verteilen, Vorahnung

Exercise 7.13

In the words in Exercise 7.12 above, place a vertical line | where a glottal separation occurs; indicate primary stress.

B. Suffixes

A suffix will *not* ordinarily be separated from a preceding element by a glottal separation; for example, in *Ahnung* [ˈaːnʊŋ] "notion," the suffix *-ung* is not preceded by a glottal separation.

C. Compounds

In a compound word, an element that begins with a vowel will normally be preceded by a glottal separation, as in *Waldeinsamkeit* ['valt͜ǀaɛnzaːmˌkaɛt] "forest solitude." It will require a fair amount of experience and some knowledge of German to understand how to divide some words.

Exercise 7.14

Pronounce the following words, using a glottal separation where necessary. The stress is on the first element, unless otherwise indicated.

1. berg'auf, jahr'ein, kläräugig, herzergreifend, Hufeisen
2. Todesahnung, liebentflammten, Blutacker, Klageruf
3. gottergeben, Götterfunken, Donnerschlag, herzerschütternd, jahr'aus
4. Liebeserklärung, Meisterehre, Abendessen, unter'dessen, Aberglaube
5. bandartig, Blasinstrument, bösartig, Drehorgel, Dreieck
6. ehrerbietig, Handarbeit, Lesart, Tonart

Exercise 7.15

In the words in Exercise 7.14 above, place a vertical line | where a glottal separation occurs.

D. Inflection

An inflectional ending will *not* normally be separated from a preceding element by a glottal separation; for example, in *bebest* ['beːbəst], there is no glottal stop before the ending *-est*.

Excerpts

Read the following excerpts aloud, paying careful attention to the use of glottal stop:

1.

Ihrem Aug' eilt Amor zu...   Her glance is quickened by love...

An Silvia
Shakespeare (Bauernfeld)/Schubert

2.

Geuß nicht so laut der liebentflammten Lieder	Don't pour so loudly (your) love-drenched song's
Tonreichen Schall	fulsome sounds
Vom Blütenast des Apfelbaums hernieder,	down from the blossoming branch of the apple tree,
O Nachtigall!	oh nightingale!

An die Nachtigall
Hölty/Brahms

3.

Ich saß zu deinen Füßen	I sat at your feet
in Waldeseinsamkeit;	in forest solitude;
Windesatmen, Sehnen	wind's breath, longing
ging durch die Wipfel breit.	swept through the broad treetops.
In stummem Ringen senkt' ich	In silent struggle I lowered
das Haupt in deinen Schoß,	my head onto your lap,
und meine bebenden Hände	and my trembling hands
um deine Knie ich schloss.	around your knees I clasped.
Die Sonne ging hinunter,	The sun went down,
der Tag verglühte all.	the day's glow faded away.
Ferne, ferne, ferne	Far off, far off, far off
sang eine Nachtigall.	sang a nightingale.

In Waldeseinsamkeit
Lemcke/Brahms

SECTION 4: DOUBLE CONSONANTS AND TIED CONSONANTS

As we have indicated, a double consonant within one element is generally pronounced the same as a single consonant: *beginnen* [bə'ɡɪnən] "begin."[14]

When one element ends with a consonant and the next element begins with the same consonant, the consonant is extended. Duden indicates this extension with two consonants: *Annahme* ['annaːmə] "assumption." Siebs uses two consonants and a tie bar: ['anːaːmə].[15]

SECTION 5: STRESS IN LOAN WORDS

There are many words in German borrowed over time from other languages—chiefly Latin, Greek, and French—in which the stress placement is at, or near, the end of the word. The following is a sampling of different word types that follow this stress pattern. (See Chapter 6 for words ending in *-ik* and Chapter 9 for words ending in *-ie*.) When such words occur in exercises in this book, we will indicate the stress, e.g. Stu'dent. Recall that, when a vowel appears in an unstressed syllable before a single consonant, it retains its quality, but is generally not long: [ʃtu'dɛnt].

Student [ʃtu'dɛnt]

Instrument [ɪnstɾu'mɛnt]

instrumental [ɪnstɾumɛn'taːl]

Pianist [pia'nɪst]

Universität [univɛɾzi'tɛːt]

Musikant [muzi'kant]

elegant [ele'ɡant]

---

[14]Both Siebs and Duden reflect this pronunciation in their transcriptions. Some singers may extend the consonant, depending on expressive intention.

[15]When consonants of similar articulation occur at the juncture of two elements, Siebs uses the tie bar to indicate that the consonant is not released until the end of the second consonant: *abblassen* ['apblasən] "fade." (Siebs, p. 26)

Melodei [melo'daɛ̯]

Appetit [ape'tiːt]

Prophet [pʀo'feːt]

General [gene'ʀaːl]

Nation [na'tsi̯oːn]

national [natsi̯o'naːl]

Minute [mi'nuːtə]

Sekunde [ze'kʊndə]

Kanone [ka'noːnə]

Kalender [ka'lɛndɐ]

Theater [te'aːtɐ]

Orchester [ɔʀ'kɛstɐ]

Charakter [ka'ʀaktɐ]

The Sounds of *b, d, g*

The consonants *b, d,* and *g*[1] are voiced: (1) when they come before a vowel that is in the same element, or (2) before *l* or *r* in the same element.

You will recall from Chapter 7 that, in general, when these consonants occur before a consonant, at the end of a word, or at the end of an element, they become unvoiced. You will also recall that when they appear before *l, n,* or *r* in inflected forms and derivatives of words ending in *-el, -en,* or *-er,* they are not usually unvoiced.

A double consonant occurring within one element usually follows the same rules for pronunciation as a single consonant.[2]

In some exercises in Chapter 7, we used the slash / to indicate a separation in the pronunciation of consonants, assuring that no blend occurs, e.g. *Zug/luft.* We will not use the slash in this and the following sections; however, the singer should remain aware that in words like *lieblich* and *abreisen, bl* and *br* do not form blends and should be pronounced with their respective elements. In many cases, indication of secondary stress can be helpful in separating consonants.

---

[1]The rules for voicing apply also to *s* (see Chapter 10).
[2]Some singers may extend the consonant, depending on expressive intention.

SECTION 1: *b, bb*

b

[b] (lower-case B)

When followed in the same element by a vowel, *l*, or *r*, the letter *b* is pronounced [b], as in *Eber* ['eːbɐ] "boar," *geblickt* [gəˈblɪkt] "glimpsed," *verbracht* [fɛɐˈbraxt] "spent" (as time). Before *l*, *n*, or *r* in an inflected form or derivative of a word ending in -*el*, -*en*, or -*er*, the *b* is considered part of the same element and is pronounced [b], as in *übler* ['yːblɐ] (<*übel*) "evil."

[p] (lower-case P)

In general, when *b* appears before a consonant, at the end of a word, or at the end of an element, it is pronounced [p]: *Liebster* ['liːpstɐ] "dearest," *Grab* [graːp] "grave," *abändern* ['abˌɛndɐn] "transform," *lieblich* ['liːpˌlɪç][3] "dear," *abreisen* ['apˌraɛzən] "depart."

Exercise 8.1

Contrast voiced and unvoiced *b* in the following pairs of related words:

1. lebe	lebt
2. grabe	gräbst
3. geben	gibt
4. halber	Halbinsel
5. leben	leblos
6. lieben	liebäugeln

bb

One Element: [b], [p]

In the few words in which *bb* occurs within the same element, it is pronounced according to the rules for *b*, for example, *Ebbe* ['ɛbə] "ebb tide," *verebbt* [fɛɐˈlɛpt] "ebbed."

Two Elements: [pb]

In most instances *bb* occurs at the junction of two elements, in which case it is pronounced [pb], as in *abbauen* ['apˌbaɔən] "dismantle." Note that the [p] is not released before proceeding to the [b].[4]

---

[3]Some singers prefer to voice these consonants before -*lich* and certain other suffixes: ['liːbˌlɪç]. (Siebs also reflects this pronunciation.)
[4]This linking is sometimes indicated with a tie bar: [p͡b] or [p͜b].

Exercise 8.2

Pronounce the following words, paying careful attention to the pronunciation of *b;* recall the rules for stress and division of elements from Chapter 7.

1. bitte, ob, ob'wohl, lobe, lobt, Lob
2. liebe, lieb, lieblich, geliebt, lieber, Liebchen, Liebschaft
3. schwebt, gibst, trübst, lebst, Leben, grubst
4. Obst, tobt, bebt, übt, Trieb, Triebe
5. Erlebnis, Trübsal, strebsam, leblos, lebhaft
6. abrennen, abbrennen, herabsehen, hinabeilen
7. vergebe, vergeblichen, geblichen, geblasen, gebt, unablässig
8. ablassen, abblassen, erblassen, 'gebet, Gebet, Verlöbnis
9. Himbeere, aberkennen, Aberglaube, Abende, Schreibpapier
10. grabe, Grab, Grabrede, Krabbe, Ebne (<eben), biblisch (<Bibel)

Exercise 8.3

Transcribe the words in Exercise 8.2 above into the IPA. (Note: *w*=[v], *ie*=[iː], *sch*=[ʃ], initial *st*=[ʃt], *v*=[f], *au*=[aʊ], *ei*=[aɛ])

Recording

Practice reading the text of the following song. Then record it without pausing.

Du meine Seele, du mein Herz,	You my soul, you my heart,
Du meine Wonn', o du mein Schmerz,	you my ecstasy, oh, you my pain,
Du meine Welt, in der ich lebe,	you my world in which I live,
Mein Himmel du, darein ich schwebe,	my heaven you, to which I soar,
O du mein Grab, in das hinab	oh, you my grave into which
Ich ewig meinen Kummer gab!	I forever placed my cares!
Du bist die Ruh, du bist der Frieden,	You are calmness, you are peace,
Du bist vom Himmel mir beschieden,	you were by heaven sent to me;
Dass du mich liebst, macht mich mir wert,	(the fact) that you love me makes me valuable to myself,
Dein Blick hat mich vor mir verklärt,	your gaze has transfigured me in my own eyes,
Du hebst mich liebend über mich,	you raise me lovingly above myself,
Mein guter Geist, mein bess'res Ich!	my good spirit, my better self!

Widmung
Rückert/R. Schumann

Song   Sing the following song, paying special attention to the pronunciation of *b*.

Ach, wie ist's möglich dann,
dass ich dich lassen kann!
Hab' dich von Herzen lieb,
das glaube mir!
Du hast die Seele mein
so ganz genommen ein,
dass ich kein' andre lieb'
als dich allein.

Blau ist ein Blümelein,
das heißt Vergissnichtmein.
Dies Blümlein leg' ans Herz
und denk an mich!
Stirbt Blüt' und Hoffnung gleich,
wir sind an Liebe reich;
Denn die stirbt nie bei mir,
das glaube mir!

Wär' ich ein Vögelein,
wollt' ich bald bei dir sein,
scheut' Falk' und Habicht nicht,
flög' schnell zu dir.
Schöss' mich ein Jäger tot,
fiel' ich in deinen Schoß;
säh'st du mich traurig an,
gern stürb' ich dann.

Oh, how is it possible then
that I can leave you!
(I) love you with all my heart,
please believe that!
This soul (of) mine you have
so completely taken
That I (can) love no other
but you alone.

Blue is a little flower,
it is called forget-me-not.
This little flower press to your heart
and think of me!
(Even if) blossom and hope die now,
we are rich in love;
because it will never die with me,
please believe that!

Were I a little bird,
(I) would want to be with you soon,
(I) would not fear falcon or hawk,
(I) would fly quickly to you.
If a hunter shot me dead,
I would fall into your lap;
if you looked at me sadly,
then I would die happy.

Ach, wie ist's möglich dann

daß   ich   kein'   an - dre   lieb'   als   dich   al - lein.
denn   die   stirbt   nie   bei   mir,   das   glau - be   mir!
säh'st   du   mich   trau - rig   an,   gern   stürb'   ich   dann.

SECTION 2: *d, dt, dd*

d

[d] (lower-case D)   When followed in the same element by a vowel or *r*, the letter *d* is pronounced [d], as in *Ader* [ˈaːdɐ] "artery," *bedrohen* [bəˈdroːən] "threaten."

Before *l*, *n*, or *r* in an inflected form or derivative of a word ending in *-el*, *-en*, or *-er*, the *d* is considered part of the same element and is pronounced [d], as in *edler* [ˈeːdlɐ] (<*edel*) "noble."

[t] (lower-case T)   In general, when *d* appears before a consonant, at the end of a word, or at the end of an element, it is pronounced [t], as in *freundlich* [ˈfrɔøntˌlɪç] "friendly," *Freund* [frɔønt] "friend," *fremdartig* [ˈfrɛmtˌaːɐ̯tɪç] "strange."

Exercise 8.4   Contrast voiced and unvoiced *d* in the following pairs of related words:

1. Lieder	Lied
2. Ende	Endergebnis
3. laden	lädst
4. Stunde	stündlich
5. Kinder	Kind
6. Erde	Erdball

dt

One Element

When the combination *dt* appears within one element, it is pronounced [t], as in *Städte* ['ʃtɛːtə] "cities."

Two Elements

If *dt* represents parts of two different elements, then it is pronounced [tt], as in *Handtuch* ['hant͜tuːx] "towel." Note that the first [t] is not released, but tied over to the second [t] and then released. This linking is sometimes indicated with a tie bar: [t͜t].

dd

One Element

In the handful of words in which *dd* occurs within the same element, it is pronounced according to the rules for *d*, as in *Widder* ['vɪdɐ] "ram."

Two Elements

Usually, *dd* represents parts of two elements and is pronounced [td], as in *Raddampfer* ['raːt͜dampfɐ] "paddle wheeler" (steamboat). Note that the [t] is not released, but tied over to the [d] and then released.[5]

Exercise 8.5

Pronounce the following words, paying attention to the rules for pronunciation of *d*. Recall the rules for stress and division of elements from Chapter 7.

1. Dame, bedacht, Feder, Verdruss, endlich, lädt
2. Band, Bande, bandartig, Bandreif, Todesbanden
3. Wildnis, endlos, Feindschaft, Mädchen, widmen, widrig
4. Waldhüter, Lindrung, Geld, seidnes, Waldeinsamkeit
5. tödlich, redlich, Redner, redselig, beredsam, golden, Gold, goldne
6. südlich, sündhaft, Abenddämmerung, verheddern
7. Erde, irdisch, Erdteil, erdreisten, huldreichstes, Handarbeit
8. Abendröte, Abendstern, Abendessen, anordnen

---

[5]This linking is sometimes indicated with a tie bar: [t͜d] or [t̯d].

Excerpts   Read the following excerpts aloud:

1.

Was vermeid' ich denn die Wege, Wo die andern Wandrer gehn ...	Why do I avoid then the paths where the other wanderers walk…

Der Wegweiser (Winterreise)
Müller/Schubert

2.

Im Felde schleich' ich still und wild, Gespannt mein Feuerrohr, Da schwebt so licht dein liebes Bild, Dein süßes Bild mir vor.	In the field I creep, quietly and eagerly, at the ready my gun, then appears so clearly your dear image, your sweet image before me.
Du wandelst jetzt wohl still und mild Durch Feld und liebes Thal, Und ach, mein schnell verrauschend Bild, Stellt sich dir's nicht einmal?	You're probably strolling now, quietly and gently, through field and beloved valley, and ah, my rapidly fading image, does it never appear before you?
Mir ist es, denk' ich nur an dich, Als in den Mond zu sehn; Ein stiller Friede kommt auf mich, Weiß nicht, wie mir geschehn.	I feel, (if) I just think about you, as (if) I were looking into the moon; a quiet peace comes upon me, (and) I don't know what (has) happened to me.

Jägers Abendlied
Goethe/Schubert, Reichardt

   3.

Ich hatt' ihn ausgeträumet, Der Kindheit friedlich schönen Traum, Ich fand allein mich, verloren Im öden, unendlichen Raum.	I had finished dreaming it, childhood's peacefully lovely dream; I found myself alone, lost in a desolate, endless space.

Du Ring an meinem Finger
Chamisso/Schumann

Song   Sing the following song, concentrating on the pronunciation of *d*.

Gold und Silber lieb' ich sehr,	Gold and silver I love very much,
Könnt' es auch gebrauchen;	I could also use them;
Hätt' ich nur ein ganzes Meer,	if I only had an entire sea (of them)
Mich hineinzutauchen.	To dive into!
'S braucht ja nicht geprägt zu sein,	It doesn't even need to be minted,
Hab' es auch sonst gerne,	I'll take it as it is,
Gleich des Mondes Silberschein	like the silver gleam of the moon
Und der gold'nen Sterne.	and of the golden stars.
Seht, wie blinkt der gold'ne Wein	See how the golden wine sparkles
Hier in meinem Becher;	here in my glass;
Hört, wie klingen silberhell	hear resounding, clear as silver,
Lieder froher Zecher.	songs of happy drinkers.
Dass die Zeit einst golden war,	That the time back then was golden
Möcht' ich nicht bestreiten,	I don't wish to deny;
Denkt man doch im Silberhaar	one thinks indeed, when one's hair is silver,
Gern vergang'ner Zeiten.	fondly of olden times.
Doch viel schöner ist das Gold,	Yet more beautiful is the gold
Das vom Lockenköpfchen	of the curls tumbling from the head
Meines trauten Liebchens rollt	of my dearest love
In zwei blonden Zöpfchen.	in two blonde little braids.
Darum fröhlich, liebes Kind,	So joyfully, dear child,
Lass uns herzen, küssen,	let us hug (and) kiss
Bis die Locken silbern sind	until those curls are silver
Und wir scheiden müssen.	and we must part.

Gold und Silber

Gold und Sil - ber lieb' ich sehr, könnt' es auch ge - brau - chen;
Seht, wie blinkt der gold' - ne Wein hier in mei - nem Be - cher;
Doch viel schö - ner ist das Gold, das vom Lok - ken - köpf - chen

hätt' ich nur ein gan - zes Meer, mich hin - ein - zu - tau - chen.
hört, wie klin - gen sil - ber - hell Lie - der fro - her Ze - cher.
mei - nes trau - ten Lieb - chens rollt in zwei blon - den Zöpf - chen.

's braucht ja nicht ge - prägt zu sein, hab' es sonst auch ger - ne
Daß die Zeit einst gol - den war, möcht' ich nicht be - strei - ten,
Dar - um fröh - lich, lie - bes Kind, laß uns her - zen, küs - sen,

gleich des Mon - des Sil - ber - schein und der gold' - nen Ster - ne,
denkt man doch im Sil - ber - haar gern ver - gang' - ner Zei - ten,
bis die Lok - ken sil - bern sind und wir schei - den müs - sen,

gleich des Mon - des Sil - ber - schein und der gold' - nen Ster - ne.
denkt man doch im Sil - ber - haar gern ver - gang' - ner Zei - ten.
bis die Lok - ken sil - bern sind und wir schei - den müs - sen.

SECTION 3: *g, ig, gn, gg*

g

[g] (lower-case G)   When followed in the same element by a vowel, *l*, or *r*, the letter *g* is pronounced [g], as in *klagen* ['klaːgən] "lament," *beglücken* [bə'glʏkən] "make happy," *begrüßen* [bə'gryːsən] "greet."

Before *l*, *n*, or *r* in an inflected form or derivative of a word ending in *-el*, *-en*, or *-er*, the *g* is considered part of the same element and is pronounced [g], as in *eigner* ['aɛgnɐ] (<*eigen*) "own."

[k] (lower-case K)   In general, when *g* appears before a consonant, at the end of a word, or at the end of an element, it is pronounced [k], as in *klagt* [klaːkt] "laments," *lag* [laːk] "lay," *kläglich* ['klɛːklɪç] "wretched," *bergab* [ˌbɛrk|ap] "downhill."

[ʒ] (ezh *or* tailed Z)   In some words of French origin, *g* is pronounced [ʒ]. Learn the following:

Genie	[ʒe'niː]	"genius"
genieren	[ʒe'niːrən]	"embarrass"
Gendarm	[ʒan'darm]	"gendarm"
Orange	[o'rãːʒə]	"orange"
Rage	['raːʒə]	"rage"
Regie	[re'ʒiː]	"direction" (theatrical)
Regisseur	[reʒi'søːɐ]	"director"
Courage	[ku'raːʒə]	"courage"
arrangieren	[arã'ʒiːrən]	"arrange"

Exercise 8.6   Contrast voiced and unvoiced *g* in the following pairs of related words:

1. lagen   lagst
2. bewegen   bewegt
3. Zuge   Zugabteil

4. mögen   möglich
5. Zeuge   Zeugnis
6. hege   hegt

ig

[ɪç]   At the end of a word or before a consonant, *-ig* is pronounced [ɪç], as in *heilig* [ˈhae̯lɪç] "holy" and *heiligt* [ˈhae̯lɪçt] "consecrates."

[ɪg]   Before a vowel, *-ig* is pronounced [ɪg], as in *heilige* [ˈhae̯lɪgə] "holy."

[ɪk]   Before a syllable ending in the sound [ç], (usually the suffix *-lich*), *-ig* is pronounced [ɪk], as in *königlich* [ˈkøːnɪkˌlɪç] "royal."

Exercise 8.7   Contrast the pronunciation of *-ig* in the following pairs of related words:

1. wichtigen   wichtig
2. lockige   lockig
3. beleidigen   beleidigt
4. ewige   Ewigkeit
5. brünstige   brünstigsten
6. wenige   wenigstens

gn

One Element   If the combination *gn* appears within one element, it is pronounced [gn], as in *Gnom* [gnoːm] "gnome."

gg

One Element   In the few words in which *gg* occurs within the same element, it is pronounced according to the rules for *g*, as in *Flagge* [ˈflagə] "flag."

Two Elements

In most instances, *gg* represents parts of two elements and is pronounced [kg], as in *weggehen* ['vɛkˌgeːən] "go away." Note that the [k] is not released before proceding to the [g].[6]

Exercise 8.8

Pronounce the following words, paying attention to the rules for the pronunciation of *g*. Recall the rules for stress and division of elements from Chapter 7.

1. lege, legst, gelegt, Belegs, legte, begleiten
2. Berg, Bergland, Berggeist, Roggen, weggetan
3. Flug, Flugs, Fluggast, flügge, zu'gleich, Zugluft
4. innig, innige, inniglich, Genie, Gene'ral, möglich
5. eigen, geeignet, begegnen, behaglich, wenigstens
6. arg, arglos, regnet, Zögling, zogst, Betrugs
7. vergnügt, Traurigkeit, segnen, brünstigsten, Bergnymphe
8. holdseliglich, kreuzigte, Heiligtum, Königreich, berg'auf
9. arglistig, jeglich, geglichen, gehegt, Gnade, Gegner
10. vergnügen, wonniglich, fügte, bewogst, heilges, sorglos

Exercise 8.9

Transcribe the words in Exercise 8.8 into the IPA. (Note: *ei*=[aɛ], *w*=[v], *z*=[ts], *v*=[f], *au*=[aʊ])

Excerpts

Read the following excerpts aloud:

1.

Es grünet ein Nussbaum vor dem Haus,	A nut tree grows green before the house;
Duftig,	fragrantly,
Luftig	airily,
Breitet er blättrig die Äste aus.	it spreads its leafy branches wide.

Der Nussbaum
Mosen/Schumann

---

[6]This linking is sometimes indicated with a tie bar: [k͡g] or [kg].

2.

Der Mond scheint hell, der Rasen grün
Ist gut zu unserm Begegnen,
Du trägst ein Schwert und nickst so kühn,
Dein' Liebschaft will ich segnen!

Und als erschien der lichte Tag,
Was fand er auf der Heide!
Ein Toter in den Blumen lag
Zu einer Falschen Leide.

The moon shines brightly, the green grass
is just right for our encounter;
you wear a sword and nod so boldly,
I'll "bless" your affair!

And when appeared the light of day,
what did it find upon the heath!
A dead man in the flowers lay,
to a faithless woman's sorrow.

Verrat
Lemcke/Brahms

3.

Als ich befriedigt,
Freudigen Herzens,
Sonst dem Geliebten im Arme lag,
Immer noch rief er,
Sehnsucht im Herzen,
Ungeduldig den heutigen Tag.

Helft mir, ihr Schwestern,
Helft mir verscheuchen
Eine thörichte Bangigkeit,
Dass ich mit klarem
Aug' ihn empfange,
Ihn, die Quelle der Freudigkeit.

As I lay contented,
with a joyful heart,
(then) in the arms of my beloved,
still he called out,
longing in his heart,
impatiently (for) this day (wedding day).

Help me, you sisters,
help me dispel
a foolish fear,
that I with clear
eyes may receive him,
him, the source of (my) happiness.

Helft mir, ihr Schwestern (Frauenliebe und -leben)
Chamisso/Schumann

4.

Durchzuckt von seligsten Genusses Schmerz,
des heiligsten Blutes Quell'
fühl' ich sich gießen in mein Herz:
des eignen sündigen Blutes Gewell'...

Convulsed by the most blessed pleasure's pain,
wellspring of the most holy blood
I can feel pouring into my heart:
the surge of my own sinful blood...

Parsifal, Act I
Wagner

Song   Sing the following song, paying special attention to the pronunciation of *g*.

Ich hatt' einen Kameraden,	I had a comrade,
einen besser'n find'st du nit.	a better (one) you'll never find.
Die Trommel schlug zum Streite,	The drumroll called (us) to battle,
er ging an meiner Seite	he walked by my side,
in gleichem Schritt und Tritt.	together step by step.
Eine Kugel kam geflogen,	A bullet came flying,
gilt sie mir oder gilt sie dir?	is it for me or is it for you?
Ihn hat es weggerissen,	It tore him away,
er liegt mir vor den Füßen,	he's lying at my feet
als wär's ein Stück von mir.	as if he were a piece of me.
Will mir die Hand noch reichen,	(He) wants to stretch out his hand to me,
derweil ich eben lad':	just as I'm reloading:
"Kann dir die Hand nicht geben,	"(I) can't take your hand—
bleib' du im ew'gen Leben	rest (you) in eternal life,
mein guter Kamerad."	my beloved comrade."

Ich hatt' einen Kameraden

Ich hatt' ei - nen Ka - me - ra - den, ei - nen bes - ser'n find'st du
Eine Ku - gel kam ge - flo - gen, gilt sie mir oder gilt sie
Will mir die Hand noch rei - chen, der - weil ich e - ben

nit. Die___ Trom - mel schlug zum Strei - te, er___
dir? Ihn___ hat es weg - ge - ris - sen, er___
lad': "Kann___ dir die Hand nicht ge - ben, bleib___

ging an mei - ner Sei - te in glei - chem Schritt und___
liegt mir vor den Fü - ßen, als wär's ein Stück von___
du im ew' - gen Le - ben mein gu - ter Ka - me -

Tritt,   in   glei - chem   Schritt   und ___   Tritt.
mir,   als   wär's   ein   Stück   von ___   mir.
rad,   mein   gu - ter   Ka   me - rad.

9

Monophthongs: Part II

In Chapter 6, general rules were stated regarding the length and quality of the vowels of that chapter: *i, ü (y), e, ö, o, u*. The vowels *a*, *ä* and *ie* were not included in Chapter 6 because they deviate from these rules somewhat.

SECTION 1: *a*

In the introduction to *Deutsche Aussprache,* Siebs states: "The distinction between a darker and a brighter *a*-sound in German is very slight and, where it occurs, determined not only by the length of the vowel. It is therefore not reflected here." (Siebs, p. 53) He also indicates that the position of *a*, which he calls a lax vowel, is not back, as for [ɑ] nor front, as for [a], but central—and then opts to use [ɑː, ɑ] in transcribing the sounds of this central *a*. (See chart, Siebs, p. 34)

Since the last edition of Siebs was published, most sources have moved to using [aː, a] to transcribe the sounds of *a*, and we will also follow this practice.

[aː] (lower-case A)

Like other long vowels, *a* is regularly pronounced long: (1) before a single consonant, as in *Amen* ['aːmɛn]; (2) before *h*, as in *ahnen* ['aːnən] "to sense"; and (3) when doubled, as in *Saal* [zaːl] "hall."

131

Exceptions

In some words, *a* is long before two or more consonants.[1] Learn the following:

1. before *ch* in:

   nach [naːx]   "after, toward"

   (*Note:* The *a* in this element is short in *Nachbar* [ˈnaxˌbaːɐ̯] "neighbor")

   brach [braːx]   "broke"

   stach [ʃtaːx]   "pricked"

   Schmach [ʃmaːx]   "disgrace"

   Sprache [ˈʃpraːxə]   "language, speech"

2. before *r* + consonant in:

   Art [aːɐ̯t]   "kind, sort"

   Bart [baːɐ̯t]   "beard"

   zart [tsaːɐ̯t]   "gentle"

   Arzt [aːɐ̯tst]   "doctor"

3. in some other words:

   Bratsche [ˈbraːtʃə]   "viola"

   atmen [ˈaːtmən]   "breathe"

   Magd [maːkt]   "maid"

   Jagd [jaːkt]   "hunt"

Note: words with ß

In accordance with the spelling rules of 1996, a vowel followed by *ß* will be long. However, depending on the source and date of the text, the spelling of a word may not reflect this rule, and the singer is advised to learn the following words with long *a*, which may occasionally appear with *ss* instead of *ß*. (See also Chapter 10.)

   Spaß [ʃpaːs]   "fun"

   saß [zaːs]   "sat"

   Straße [ˈʃtraːsə]   "street"

   Maß [maːs]   "measure"

---

[1]Normally, *a* is short before *ch*, *r* + consonant, and *ss*, as expected.

(Note that *a* is short, as expected, in *dass* "that," also spelled *daß* in older texts)

Exercise 9.1   Pronounce:

1. Staat, fragen, Mahl, Ba'nane, Trübsal
2. Kahn, Grab, prahlen, fragt, labt

[a]

The pronunciation of *a* is regularly short [a] before two or more consonants, as in *Macht* [maxt] "power."

Exceptions   In some words, *a* is pronounced short before a single consonant. Learn the following:

1. short words:

an [an]	"to, at"

(and its many compounds, such as *heran* [hɛ'ran], *hinan* [hɪ'nan])

am [am]	"to the, at the"
ab [ap]	"away"

(and its many compounds, such as *herab* [hɛ'rap], *hinab* [hɪ'nap])

man [man]	"one, someone"
das [das]	"that, the"
was [vas]	"what"
hat [hat]	"has"
hast [hast]	(you) "have"

2. other words:

Monat ['moːnat]	"month"
Heimat ['haemat]	"home"
Bräutigam ['brɔøtɪgam]	"groom"

Exercise 9.2

Contrast [aː] and [a] in the following pairs:

1.	Maße	Masse
2.	Saat	satt
3.	Staat	Stadt
4.	Schlaf	schlaff
5.	Haken	Hacken
6.	kam	Kamm
7.	Kahn	kann
8.	rast	Rast
9.	nagt	nackt

The English-speaking singer should be especially careful about the pronunciation of *a* in unstressed syllables. Although the pronunciation of unstressed *a* is reduced to [ə] in English, as in *America* [ə'mɛɹɪkə], in German the pronunciation is clearly an a-sound, as in *Amerika* [a'meːɾɪka], Schumann ['ʃuːman]. The unstressed prefix *da-*, as in *dafür* [da'fyːɐ̯] tends to be particularly troublesome for the English-speaking student.

Exercise 9.3

Pronounce:

1. Monat, Tag, Gasse, wandern, schwarz
2. fragen, sagt, Abend, barfuß, wach
3. Bach, ach, machen, Schmach, brach
4. Blatt, Hand, Nachtigall, Wahn, sahen
5. Karte, Pappeln, nass, saß, Wasser
6. fahle, falle, sanft, alles, fragt
7. Schumann, Telemann, Richard

Exercise 9.4

Transcribe the words in Exercise 9.3 into the IPA. (Note: *w*=[v]; *sch*=[ʃ]; prevocalic *s*=[z])

Excerpts   1.

Nun hast du mir den ersten Schmerz getan,
Der aber traf.
Du schläfst, du harter, unbarmherz'ger Mann,
Den Todesschlaf.

Now you have caused me my first pain,
which really hurt.
You sleep, you hard, merciless man,
the sleep of death.

Frauenliebe und -leben
Chamisso/Schumann

   2.

Um Mitternacht
hab' ich gedacht
hinaus in dunkle Schranken.
Es hat kein Lichtgedanken
mir Trost gebracht
um Mitternacht.

At midnight
my thoughts wandered
out into dark places.
No bright thoughts
brought me comfort
at midnight.

Um Mitternacht
Rückert/Mahler

3.

Ich unglücksel'ger Atlas! Eine Welt,
Die ganze Welt der Schmerzen, muss ich tragen.
Ich trage Unerträgliches, und brechen
Will mir das Herz im Leibe.

I, unfortunate Atlas! A world,
the whole world of pain, must I carry.
I bear (the) unbearable, and break—
my heart will (break) inside my body.

Der Atlas
Heine/Schubert

4.

Allein und abgetrennt
von aller Freude,
seh' ich ans Firmament
nach jener Seite.

Alone and cut off
from all joy,
I gaze to the heavens,
in that direction.

Lied der Mignon
Goethe/Schubert

Song   Sing the following song, concentrating on the pronunciation of *a*.

Das Wandern ist des Müllers Lust,	Wandering is the miller's delight,
Das Wandern!	wandering!
Das muss ein schlechter Müller sein,	It must be a poor miller
Dem niemals fiel das Wandern ein,	to whom wandering never occurred,
Das Wandern.	wandering!
Vom Wasser haben wir's gelernt,	From the water we have learned it,
Vom Wasser!	from the water!
Das hat nicht Ruh' bei Tag und Nacht,	It has no rest by day or night,
Ist stets auf Wanderschaft bedacht,	is ever bent on wandering,
Das Wasser.	the water.
Das seh'n wir auch den Rädern ab,	We learn it too from the mill wheels,
Den Rädern!	the mill wheels!
Die gar nicht gerne stille steh'n	Which don't like at all to be still,
Und sich bei Tag nicht müde dreh'n,	and weary not of turning all day,
Die Räder.	the mill wheels.
O Wandern, Wandern, meine Lust,	Oh wandering, wandering, my delight,
O Wandern!	oh wandering!
Herr Meister und Frau Meisterin,	Oh, Master and Mistress,
Lasst mich in Frieden weiter zieh'n	let me move on in peace
Und wandern.	and wander.

Wanderschaft

Recording   Practice reading the text of the previous song. Then record it without pausing.

SECTION 2: *ä*

[ɛː] (epsilon)

In singing, *ä* is pronounced as an open vowel even if it is long: [ɛː].[2] It is generally pronounced long before a single consonant, as in *spät* [ʃpɛːt] "late," and before *h*, as in *Mähne* ['mɛːnə] "mane."

Exceptions   In some words, *ä* is long before two or more consonants. Learn the following:

Gemälde [gə'mɛːldə]	"painting"
Rätsel ['rɛːtsəl]	"riddle"
Städte ['ʃtɛːtə]	"cities"
zärtlich ['tsɛːɐ̯t͜lɪç]	"gentle"
Gespräch [gə'ʃprɛːx]	"conversation"

Note: words with *ß*

In accordance with the spelling rules of 1996, a vowel followed by *ß* will be long. However, depending on the source and date of the text, the spelling of a word may not reflect this rule, and the singer is advised to learn the following words with long *ä*, which may occasionally appear with *ss* instead of *ß*. (See also Chapter 10.)

mäßig ['mɛːsɪç]	"moderate"
säße ['zɛːsə]	"would sit"
Späße ['ʃpɛːsə]	"jokes"

---

[2]In speaking, long *ä* is frequently pronounced as closed [eː]; but this pronunciation should be avoided in singing.

[ɛ]

The pronunciation of *ä* is regularly short before two or more consonants, as in *Händel* ['hɛndəl].

Exercise 9.5   Contrast long and short ä in the following pairs:

1. stähle	Ställe
2. lähme	Lämmer
3. Städte	Stätte
4. läst	lässt
5. bäte	Bette
6. Hähne	Henne

Exercise 9.6   Pronounce the following words containing *ä*:

1. Händel, Götterdämmerung, Ländler, Bäcker
2. Jäger, Hähne, Mädchen, krähen, erklärt
3. dämpfen, ändern, ängstlich, Ärger, fährt
4. Bäche, lästern, Verräter, Blätter, Nächte
5. jähes, Ähre, Träne, Märchen, grämlich

Excerpts   Read the following excerpts aloud:

1.

Väter, lasst euch's Warnung sein,	Fathers, let it be a warning to you,
sperrt die Zuckerplätzchen ein!	lock up the sugar cookies!
sperrt die jungen Mädchen ein!	Lock up the young girls!

Warnung
Unknown/Mozart

2.

Du Doppelgänger, du bleicher Geselle!	You, (my) double, you pale companion,
Was äffst du nach mein Liebesleid,	why do you mimic the heartache
Das mich gequält auf dieser Stelle	that tormented me on this spot
So manche Nacht, in alter Zeit?	so many a night in times past?

Der Doppelgänger
Heine/Schubert

3.

Ängste, quäle	Frighten, torment
Dich nicht länger, meine Seele!	yourself no longer, my soul!
Freu dich! schon sind da und dorten	Be happy! Already here and there have
Morgenglocken wach geworden.	morning bells awakened.

In der Frühe
Mörike/Wolf

Song   Sing the following song, paying close attention to the pronunciation of *ä*.

Die Gedanken sind frei,	Thoughts are free,
Wer kann sie erraten,	who can guess them?
Sie fliehen vorbei	They fly past
Wie nächtliche Schatten.	like night shadows.
Kein Mensch kann sie wissen,	No one can know them,
Kein Jäger erschießen,	no hunter can shoot them,
Es bleibet dabei:	(and so) it remains:
Die Gedanken sind frei.	thoughts are free.
Ich denke was ich will	I think what I want
Und was mich beglücket,	and whatever pleases me,
Doch alles in der Still',	but all (this) in quiet,
Und wie es sich schicket.	and as is proper.
Mein Wunsch, mein Begehren	My wishing, my longing
Kann niemand mir wehren,	can no one else hinder,
Es bleibet dabei:	(and) so it remains:
Die Gedanken sind frei!	thoughts are free!
Drum will ich auf immer	So I want for ever
Den Sorgen entsagen	to give up worries
Und will mich auch nimmer	and I want no more
Mit Grillen mehr plagen.	to torment myself with problems.
Man kann ja im Herzen	One can, in one's heart,
Stets lachen und scherzen	always laugh and joke
Und denken dabei:	and think while doing so:
Die Gedanken sind frei!	Thoughts are free!

Die Gedanken sind frei

Die Ge - dan - ken sind __ frei! Wer __ kann sie er -
Ich den - ke was ich will, und __ was mich be -
Ich lie - be den __ Wein, mein __ Mäd - chen vor
Drum will ich auf __ im - mer den Sor - gen ent -

ra - ten? Sie flie - hen vor - bei wie __ nächt - li - che
glük - ket, doch al - les in der Still' und __ wie es sich
al - len, sie tut mir al - lein am __ be - sten ge -
sa - gen und will mich auch __ nim - mer mit __ Gril - len mehr

Schat - ten. Kein Mensch kann sie wis - sen, kein Jä - ger er -
schik - ket. Mein Wunsch, mein Be - geh - ren kann nie - mand mir
fal - len. Ich sitz' nicht al - lei - ne bei mei - nem Glas
pla - gen. Man kann ja im Her - zen stets la - chen und

schie - ßen,	es	blei - bet	da	-	bei:	die	Ge	-	dan	-	ken	sind	frei.
weh - ren,	es	blei - bet	da	-	bei:	die	Ge	-	dan	-	ken	sind	frei.
Wei - ne,	mein	Mäd - chen	da	-	bei:	die	Ge	-	dan	-	ken	sind	frei.
scher - zen	und	den - ken	da	-	bei:	die	Ge	-	dan	-	ken	sind	frei.

SECTION 3: *ie*

[iː] (lower-case I)

Except under the conditions outlined below, *ie* is pronounced [iː], as in *die* [diː] "the," *fliegen* ['fliːɡən] "fly." Thus it is long and closed even before more than one consonant, as in *Biest* [biːst] "beast."[3]

Exceptions

ie is pronounced short and open in:

vierzehn ['fɪrtseːn]   "fourteen"

vierzig ['fɪrtsɪç]   "forty"

Viertel ['fɪrtəl]   "quarter"

A. Final *-ie*

1. [iː]

In some words of foreign origin (usually Greek), final *-ie* is stressed and pronounced [iː], as in *Melodie* [meloˈdiː]. Many of these words are scientific, such as *Geographie, Philosophie.* However, the singer should become familiar with the following examples:

---

[3]*ie* is pronounced short and closed (in an unstressed syllable) in *vielleicht* [fiˈlaɛçt] "perhaps"

Elegie	Partie
Galerie	Phantasie
Genie	Poesie
Melancholie	Symphonie
Melodie	

2. [i̯ə]

In other words of foreign origin (usually Latin), final -ie is unstressed and pronounced [i̯ə], as in *Familie* [faˈmiːli̯ə]. The symbol [i̯] is considered nonsyllabic, that is, it is pronounced together with the following vowel.[4] The singer should learn to recognize the following words of this type:

Aˈkazie	Horˈtensie
Arie[4]	Hostie
Bestie	Kaˈmelie
Dahlie	Kaˈstanie
Faˈmilie	Koˈmödie
Fuchsie	Lilie[4]
Garˈdenie	Linie[4]
Glorie[4]	Pinie
Grazie	Traˈgödie
Hiˈstorie[4]	

B. Final *-ien*

1. [iːən]

In the plurals of words of the type *Melodie*, final -ien is pronounced [iːən], and the stress is on the next to last syllable: *Melodien* [meloˈdiːən].

2 [i̯ən]

In the plurals of words of the type *Familie*, the stress falls on the same syllable as in the singular, and final -ien is pronounced [i̯ən]: *Familien* [faˈmiːli̯ən]. Also in geographical names, -ien is pronounced

---

[4]In some words, Siebs (p. 69) considers this sound syllabic and transcribes it accordingly: *Lilie* [ˈliːliə], *Linie* [ˈliːniə]. After *r,* the sound is generally syllabic: *Arie* [ˈaːriə], *Glorie* [ˈgloːriə].

[i̯ən], for example, *Belgien* ['bɛlgi̯ən]. The following examples might occur in vocal literature:

Asien

Belgien

Indien

Italien

Spanien

Exercise 9.7   Pronounce the following words:

1. Lied, fließen, riechen, Ziel, stu'dieren

2. Kastanien, Melodien, verdient, Lilien, fliehen

3. Spanien, Symphonie, pro'bieren, Begierde, Brief

4. Partie, Riemen, wieder, Priester

5. liegen, Pinien, liebt, hielt, hier, schrie

Excerpts   Read the following excerpts aloud:

1.

Die Rose, die Lilie, die Taube, die Sonne, Die liebt' ich einst alle in Liebeswonne.	The rose, the lily, the dove, the sun, I once loved them all with love's ecstasy.

Dichterliebe
Heine/R. Schumann

2.

Erzeugt von heißer Phantasie, In einer schwärmerischen Stunde zur Welt gebrachte, Geht zu Grunde, ihr Kinder der Melancholie!	Conceived by passionate fantasy, in a rapturous hour brought into the world, go to (your) ruin, you children of melancholy!

Als Luise die Briefe
Baumberg/Mozart

Recording

Practice reading the lyrics of the following song. Then record them without pausing.

Rosen brach ich nachts mir am dunklen Hage;	Roses I picked by night from the dark hedge;
Süßer hauchten Duft sie als je am Tage;	more sweetly they exuded fragrance than ever by day;
Doch verstreuten reich die bewegten Äste	yet richly the jostled twigs scattered
Tau, der mich nässte.	dew, which moistened me.
Auch der Küsse Duft mich wie nie berückte,	And the fragrance of kisses thrilled me as never (before)
Die ich nachts vom Strauch deiner Lippen pflückte;	that I picked by night from the rosebush of your lips;
Doch auch dir, bewegt im Gemüt gleich jenen,	yet for you too, stirred in your soul like those (roses),
Tauten die Tränen!	the tears fell like dew.

Sapphische Ode
Schmidt/Brahms

10

The Sounds of *s* and
Its Combinations

SECTION 1: *s, ß, ss*

s

[z] (lower-case Z)

Before a vowel, *s* is pronounced [z], as in *singen* ['zɪŋən] "sing,"
einsam ['aɛn̩zaːm] "lonely." When *s* occurs before *l*, *n*, or *r* in an
inflected form or derivative of a word ending in *-el*, *-en*, or *-er*, it is
pronounced [z], as in *unsre* ['ʊnzɾə] *(<unser)* "our."

Exceptions

In a few words, *s* is voiceless after a voiceless (or unvoiced)
consonant, even though it precedes a vowel. Learn to recognize
the following:

Erbse ['ɛrpsə]	"pea"
Krebse ['kreːpsə]	"crabs"
Rätsel ['rɛːtsəl]	"riddle"

[s] (lower-case S)

When *s* appears before a consonant (see Section 2 for *sp* and *st*), at
the end of a word, or at the end of an element, it is pronounced [s],
as in *Dresden* ['dreːsdən], *Betrugs* [bə'truːks] "(of) deceit," *Lesart*
['leːsˌaːɐt] "version," *Grashalm* ['graːsˌhalm][1] "blade of grass."

---

[1]Note that in German, *s* and *h* do not form a combination as in English. When they
appear together, they always represent parts of two different elements and are thus
pronounced as [s] + [h].

147

Exercise 10.1

Contrast voiced and unvoiced *s* in the following pairs of related words:

1. kreisen	Kreis
2. Halse	Hals
3. Speise	speist
4. Hause	Haus
5. lösen	löst
6. lesen	lesbar

Exercise 10.2

Pronounce the following words, observing the rules for pronunciation of s:

1. Sage, Wiese, böse, Schicksal, seltsam
2. dies, diesen, Jesus, als, Felsen, kraus
3. gesät, Glas, Abendsonne, löst, Amsel, Friedenshaus
4. Hungersnot, Feins'lieb, Königs, Guts, Rose, Linse
5. Ratsherrn, Frühlingsabendrot, heisre, holdselig
6. gesund, rings'um, losgebe, Mannsbild, A'syl
7. auserkorn, Himmelslust, boshaft, Hausarzt, Röslein
8. Todesangst, Gotteserde, gottselig, Insel, Rätsel, emsige

ß

The German character *ß* is always pronounced [s]. The character is traditionally called *Eszett*[2]— the names of the letters *s* and *z* combined; it grew out of a fusion of those two letters (in Fraktur type, ſ + ʒ = ß). In older scores, *ß* may appear as *sz;* the pronunciation will remain [s], as in *auszen* ['aʊsən] (provided, of course, that *s* and *z* do not belong to two different elements, as in *Auszug* ['aʊs,tsuːk]).

We pointed out in Chapter 6 that, according to the new spelling rules adopted in 1996, the character *ß* is to appear only after a long vowel.[3] Since *ß* is a single consonant, this usage conforms to our

---

[2]The character *ß* is also called *scharfes s* ("sharp *s* ").
[3]*ß* also appears after *ie* and the diphthongs because they are long vowels, for example: *fließen* ['fliːsən] "to flow," *heiß* [haɛs] "hot," *Strauß* [ʃtraʊs] "bouquet," *Sträuße* [ʃtrɔɡsə] "bouquets," *heute* ['hɔɡtə] "today."

rule for length. However, depending on the source and date of the song text, the use of the character *ß* is not consistent. In some texts it is not used at all, and in others it may appear in alternation with *ss*. (See old spelling rules below.)[4] For that reason, in Chapters 6 and 9 we have provided lists of words containing a long vowel before this character, which we recommended learning for recognition: *büßen, Buße, Größe, groß, mäßig, Maß*, etc. In the exercises and song texts of this chapter, we will include examples taken from the literature that reflect the older usage; so the singer must be able to recognize the words from these lists.

ss

One Element

If *ss* appears in one element, it is pronounced [s], as in *müssen* ['mʏsən] "must."

Two Elements

If an element ending in *s* is followed by an element beginning with *s*, the first *s* is not voiced because it occurs at the end of an element. The second *s* is pronounced according to the conditions in the second element: *Aussage* ['aͻsˌzaːɡə] "statement," *aussteigen* ['aͻsˌʃtaͤɡən] "get off." (See also Sections 2 and 3 below.)

Exercise 10.3

Contrast *s* and *ss* (or *ß*) in the following pairs:

1. Fliesen   fließen
2. Weise   weiße
3. Nase   nasse
4. Rose   Rosse

---

[4]According to the former rules, the character *ß* is used: (1) at the end of a word or element, as in *muß* [mʊs] "must," *Gruß* [ɡruːs] "greeting," *Gußeisen* ['ɡʊsˌaͤzən] "cast iron"; (2) before a consonant, as in *müßte* ['mʏstə] "would have to," *grüßte* ['ɡryːstə] "greeted"; (3) intervocalically after a *long* vowel, as in *grüßen* ['ɡryːsən] "to greet."

From these rules we see that the only place *ss* appears is intervocalically after a short vowel, as in *müssen* ['mʏsən]. Otherwise—that is, in positions 1 and 2 above—the *ß* reveals *nothing* about the length of the preceding vowel since *ß* (not *ss*) is always written finally or before a consonant.

Exercise 10.4

Pronounce the following pairs of words, noting the contrast in the vowels preceding *ß* and *ss:*

1.	Maße	Masse
2.	hießen	hissen
3.	Schloßen	schlossen
4.	Flöße	flösse
5.	Buße	Busse
6.	rußen	Russen

Exercise 10.5

Pronounce the following words, observing the rules for pronunciation of *ß* and *ss* (these examples follow old spelling rules):

1. Wasser, essen, vermissen, draußen, heißen
2. müssen, muß, mußte, müßte, fließen
3. grüßen, Gruß, grüßte, süß, süße, Füße, Flüsse
4. Geheimnisse, Waldessaume, das'selbe, besessen
5. Aussätzigen, fesselte, weissagen, miß'achten
6. lossagen, Drossel, Liebessehnsucht, Mißverständnis

Excerpts

Read the following excerpts aloud:

1.

Allnächtlich im Traume seh' ich dich,	Every night in a dream I see you,
Und sehe dich freundlich grüßen,	and see you greet (me) warmly,
Und laut aufweinend stürz' ich mich	and, weeping loudly, I throw myself
Zu deinen süßen Füßen.	at your sweet feet.

Allnächtlich im Traume
Heine/Schumann

2.

Ich saß zu deinen Füßen
in Waldeseinsamkeit;
Windesatmen, Sehnen
ging durch die Wipfel breit.

In stummem Ringen senkt' ich
das Haupt in deinen Schoß,
und meine bebenden Hände
um deine Knie ich schloss.

Die Sonne ging hinunter,
der Tag verglühte all.
Ferne, ferne, ferne
sang eine Nachtigall.

I sat at your feet
in forest solitude;
wind's breath, longing
swept through the broad treetops.

In silent struggle I lowered
my head onto your lap,
and my trembling hands
around your knees I clasped.

The sun went down,
the day's glow faded away.
Far off, far off, far off
sang a nightingale.

In Waldeseinsamkeit
Lemcke/Brahms

Song   Sing the following song, paying close attention to the pronunciation of *s*.

Wir sind jung, die Welt ist offen,	We are young, the world is open,
O du schöne, weite Welt!	oh, you beautiful, wide world!
Unsre Sehnsucht, unser Hoffen	Our longing, our hoping
Zieht hinaus in Wald und Feld.	lead (us) out into forest and field.
Bruder, lass den Kopf nicht hängen,	Brother, don't let your head hang,
Kannst ja nicht die Sterne seh'n!	(then) you can't see the stars!
Aufwärts blicken, vorwärts drängen!	Look upward, press forward!
Wir sind jung und das ist schön!	We are young and that is good!
Liegt dort hinter jenem Walde	Is there beyond that forest
Nicht ein fernes, fremdes Land?	not a distant, foreign land?
Blüht auf grüner Bergeshalde	Blooms on the green hillside
Nicht das Blümlein unbekannt?	not an unknown flower?
Lasst uns schreiten im Gelände,	Let us stride through the landscape,
Über Täler, über Höh'n!	over valleys, over hills!
Wo sich auch der Weg hinwende:	Wherever the path leads:
Wir sind jung und das ist schön!	We are young and that is good!
Auf denn, auf! die Sonne zeige	Away then, away! May the sun show
Uns den Weg durch Wald und Hain;	us the way through forest and grove;
Geht der Tag darob zur Neige,	if the daylight fades then,
Leuchte uns der Sterne Schein.	let the stars' gleam give us light.
Bruder, schnell den Rucksack über,	Brother, quick, put on your backpack,
Heute soll's ins Weite geh'n.	today we're going far.
Regen? Wind? Wir lachen drüber:	Rain? Wind? We'll laugh at them:
Wir sind jung und das ist schön!	We are young and that is good!

Wir sind jung

Wir sind jung, die Welt ist of - fen, o du schö - ne, wei - te
Liegt dort hin - ter je - nem Wal - de nicht ein fer - nes, frem - des
Auf denn, auf! die Son - ne zei - ge uns den Weg durch Wald und

Welt! Uns - re Sehn - sucht, un - ser Hof - fen zieht hin -
Land? Blüht auf grü - ner Ber - ges - hal - de nicht das
Hain; geht der Tag dar - ob zur Nei - ge, leuch - te

aus in Wald und Feld. Bru - der, laß den Kopf nicht
Blüm - lein un - be - kannt? Laßt uns schrei - ten im Ge -
uns der Ster - ne Schein. Bru - der, schnell den Ruck - sack

hän - gen, kannst ja nicht die Ster - ne seh'n! Auf - wärts
län - de, ü - ber Tä - ler ü - ber Höh'n! Wo sich
ü - ber, heu - te soll's ins Wei - te geh'n. Re - gen?

blik - ken, vor - wärts drän - gen! Wir sind jung und das ist schön!
auch der Weg hin - wen - de: Wir sind jung und das ist schön!
Wind? wir la - chen drü - ber: Wir sind jung und das ist schön!

SECTION 2: *st, sp*

One Element

1. [ʃt, ʃp]

When *st* and *sp* appear at the beginning of a word or element, they are pronounced [ʃt, ʃp], as in *stellen* [ˈʃtɛlən] "to place," *versprechen* [fɛɐ̯ˈʃpʁɛçən] "to promise."

Exercise 10.6

Pronounce the following words:

1. stellen, Stück, aufstellen, verstehen, Gestalt
2. spinnen, Sprache, aufspalten, versprechen, Gespenst

Exceptions

1. The superlative suffix *-st-* is pronounced [st], even though it appears at the beginning of an element, regardless of what ending follows: *schnellste* [ˈʃnɛlstə], *schnellstes* [ˈʃnɛlstəs] "fastest."
2. The second person verb ending *-st* is always pronounced [st]: *du sagst*, [zaːkst] *du gehst* [geːst] "you say," "you go."

2. [st, sp]

In all other cases, *st* and *sp* are pronounced [st, sp]. Specifically, they are [st] and [sp] when they appear in one element in any position other than at the beginning, as in *beste* [ˈbɛstə] "best," *ist* [ɪst] "is."

Two Elements

If *st* and *sp* occur at the junction of two elements, then each letter will be pronounced with its element, as in *austragen* [ˈaʊ̯sˌtʁaːɡən] "carry out," *ausprägen* [ˈaʊ̯sˌpʁɛːɡən] "stamp."

Exercise 10.7

Pronounce the following words:

1. Liste, Westen, austeilen, wärmste, wärmsten
2. Wespe, Espe, auspacken, Liebespaar

Exercise 10.8

Contrast [st] and [sp] in words of similar appearance:

1. Gestirn   gestern
2. bestehen   besten
3. erstehen   ersten

Exercise 10.9

Pronounce the words below, following the rules for pronunciation of *st* and *sp*. Recall rules for stress and division of elements from Chapter 7. Note: *z*=[ts], *ei*, *ai*=[aɛ], *w*=[v], *v*=[f], *au*=[aǫ]

1. stehen, spät, entstehen, besprechen, zustoßen
2. lispeln, rasten, finster, Meister, schnellste
3. Strand, löste, schlugst, zu'erst, Saitenspiel
4. hinsterbend, bestrebt, bester, hineinstehlen, Ostern
5. erspähen, feste, Festung, sturmestot, wegstehlen
6. liebestrunkene, Waldstrom, sternebesäeten, betrügst
7. strömt, speist, Liebeston, fernste, Wanderstab, Trost
8. unheiligster, Wehmutsstrahlen, Dienstag, Diebstahl, Fenster
9. Todestag, durchspielen, seligsten, Edelstein, erstreiten
10. Versuchungsplagen, einstürzen, Waldespracht, Hammerstreich
11. huldreichstes, Liebestraum, Festrede, Garnstricker, Gaststätte
12. Gesangstunde, Gestade, gestern, gestehen, Gerstenstange
13. garstig, Gottestisch, Götterspeise, Grabstein, Fistelstimme
14. heraustritt, Himmelstrank, Singestuhl, Singstunde, desto
15. Abendstern, Muster, Austausch, austreiben, Beständigkeit
16. Baumstamm, Beispiel, Bernstein, Betstunde, schönster, düster
17. Ruhestätte, Todesstoß, Künstler, Todespein, Siegespreis

Excerpts   Read the following excerpts aloud:

1.

Und zu dem Strand, dem weiten, wogenblauen,
Werden wir still und langsam niedersteigen.

And to the shore, the wide, wave-blue (shore)
we will silently and slowly descend.

Morgen
Mackay/Strauß

2.

In deine Decke grab' ich
Mit einem spitzen Stein
Den Namen meiner Liebsten
Und Stund' und Tag hinein.

Into your (icy) surface I carve
with a sharp stone
the name of my beloved
and the hour and the day.

Auf dem Flusse
Müller/Schubert

3.

Wie anders hast du mich empfangen,
Du Stadt der Unbeständigkeit!
An deinen blanken Fenstern sangen
Die Lerch' und Nachtigall im Streit.

How differently did you receive me,
you fickle city!
At your gleaming windows sang
lark and nightingale in competition.

Rückblick
Müller/Schubert

4.

Sahst du sie gestern Abend nicht am Tore stehn,

Mit langem Halse nach der großen Straße sehn?
Wenn von dem Fang der Jäger lustig zieht nach Haus,
Da steckt kein sittsam Kind den Kopf zum Fenster
'naus.

Did you not see her yesterday evening standing at
the gate,
with her neck craned to see the main road?
When from the hunt the hunter merrily comes home,
no well-bred girl sticks her head out the window!

Eifersucht und Stolz
Müller/Schubert

5.

Zwar ist solche Herzensstube	It's true: the heart's chamber is
Wohl kein schöner Fürstensaal,	indeed no fine princely hall,
Sondern eine finstre Grube;	but rather a dark pit;
Doch, sobald dein Gnadenstrahl	yet, once your beam of grace
In dieselbe nur wird blinken,	into this place will shine,
Wird sie voller Sonnen dünken.	it will be as though filled with suns.

Weihnachtsoratorium
Bach

SECTION 3: *sch*

One Element: [ʃ] (esh)

When *sch* appears in one element, it is pronounced [ʃ], as in *Schule* [ˈʃuːlə] "school," *schräg* [ʃrɛːk] "crooked," *rasch* [raʃ] "quickly."

Two Elements

When *s* and *ch* appear together as parts of two different elements, they will, of course, be pronounced separately. In this situation, *s* appears at the end of one element and is unvoiced [s]. Usually, the following element will be the diminutive sufflx *-chen*, and *ch* will be pronounced [ç], as in *Röschen* [ˈrøːsçən] "little rose."

Exercise 10.10

Pronounce the following words, recalling the rules for pronunciation of *s* and *sch:*

1. Schiff, schmal, schlugst, Kirsche, Kirche
2. löschen, frischem, Häschen, herrschen, Dornröschen
3. Herrschaft, Austausch, ausschwärmen, Glasscherbe
4. Bläschen, Lieschen, Geschichte, Gotteshaus, Esche
5. dreschen, verschmelzen, Grashalm, boshaft, durchschleichen

Exercise 10.11   Read the following transcription aloud:

[ǀax, ǀɪç fyːls, ǀɛs ǀɪst fɛɐ̯ˈʃvʊndən,

ˈǀeːvɪç hɪn deːɐ̯ ˈliːbə glʏk.

ˈnɪmɐ kɔmt ǀiːɐ̯ ˈvɔnəʃtʊndən

ˈmaɐ̯nəm ˈhɛɐtsən meːɐ̯ tsuˈrʏk.

ziː, taˈmiːno, ˈdiːzə ˈtrɛːnən ˈfliːsən,

ˈtraɒtɐ, diːɐ̯ ǀaˈlaɛn.

fyːlst du nɪçt deːɐ̯ ˈliːbə ˈzeːnən,

zoː vɪrt ruː ǀɪm ˈtoːdə zaɛn.]

SECTION 4:
s + OTHER
CONSONANTS

The pronunciation of initial *st*, *sp*, and *sch* are discussed in the previous sections. When initial *s* is followed by other consonants, the pronunciation of *s* will generally be [s], as in: *Skandal* [skanˈdaːl] "scandal," *Smaragd* [smaˈrakt] "emerald," *Szene* [ˈstseːnə] "scene," *Sphäre* [ˈsfɛːrə] "sphere, domain," *Skizze* [ˈskɪtsə] "sketch," *slawisch* [ˈslaːvɪʃ] "Slavic."

Excerpts   Read the following excerpts aloud, paying special attention to the sounds of *s* and its combinations:

1.

O liebliche Wangen, ihr macht mir Verlangen,	O lovely cheeks, you cause me longing!
Dies Rote, dies Weiße zu schauen mit Fleiße.	This red one, this white one, to look (at them) greedily.
Und dies nur alleine ist's nicht, was ich meine;	And just this alone isn't what I mean;
Zu schauen, zu grüßen, zu rühren, zu küssen!	to look, to greet, to touch, to kiss!
O Sonne der Wonne! O Wonne der Sonne!	Oh sun of ecstasy! Oh ecstasy of the sun!
O Augen, so saugen das Licht meiner Augen.	Oh eyes, just drink in the light of my eyes.
O englische Sinnen! O himmlisch Beginnen!	Oh angelic senses! Oh heavenly beginning!
O Himmel auf Erden, magst du mir nicht werden!	Oh heaven on earth, won't you be that for me!
O Schönste der Schönen, benimm mir dies Sehnen,	Oh fairest of the fair, relieve me of this longing,
Komm, eile, komm, komme, du Süße, du Fromme!	come, hurry, come, come, you sweet (one), you pious (one)!
Ach Schwester, ich sterbe, ich sterb', ich verderbe,	Oh, Sister, I'm dying, I'm dying, I'll perish,
Komm, komme, komm, eile, benimm mir dies Sehnen,	come, come, come, hurry, relieve me of this longing,
O Schönste der Schönen!	oh fairest of the fair!

Liebliche Wangen
Fleming/Brahms

2.

O du, für den ich alles trug,	Oh you for whom I have borne everything,
Könnt' ich zur Stelle dringen,	could I (but) get to the place
Wo Bosheit dich in Fesseln schlug,	where Evil put you in chains
Und süßen Trost dir bringen!	and bring you sweet comfort!

Fidelio
Beethoven

Recording

Practice reading the text of the following song. Then record it without pausing.

3.

Meine Liebe ist grün wie der Fliederbusch,	My love is green like the lilac bush,
Und mein Lieb ist schön wie die Sonne;	and my sweetheart is lovely as the sun;
Die glänzt wohl herab auf den Fliederbusch	it shines down onto the lilac bush
Und füllt ihn mit Duft und mit Wonne.	and fills it with fragrance and with rapture.
Meine Seele hat Schwingen der Nachtigall	My soul has wings like the nightingale
Und wiegt sich in blühendem Flieder,	and nestles in the blossoming lilac,
Und jauchzet und singet vom Duft berauscht	and rejoices and sings, intoxicated by the scent,
Viel liebestrunkene Lieder.	many love-drunk songs.

Meine Liebe ist grün
Felix Schumann/Brahms

Song   Sing the following song, paying special attention to the pronunciation of *s* and its combinations.

Wem Gott will rechte Gunst erweisen,	(The one) to whom God wants to show His favor,
Den schickt er in die weite Welt,	He sends (out) into the wide world,
Dem will er seine Wunder weisen	to that one He will show His wonders
In Berg und Tal und Strom und Feld.	in mountain and valley and stream and field.
Die Bächlein von den Bergen springen,	The brooklets spring forth from the mountains,
Die Lerchen schwirren hoch vor Lust.	the larks soar high with delight.
Wie sollt' ich nicht mit ihnen singen	How could I not sing with them
Aus voller Kehl' und frischer Brust.	at the top of my lungs and with renewed spirit!
Den lieben Gott lass' ich nur walten.	The dear Lord I'll let be in charge.
Der Bächlein, Lerchen, Wald und Feld	(He) who preserves brooks, larks, forest and field
Und Erd' und Himmel will erhalten,	and earth and sky
Hat auch mein' Sach' aufs best' bestellt.	has also done well by me!

Wem Gott will rechte Gunst

Wem Gott will rech - te Gunst er - wei - sen, den
Die Bäch - lein von den Ber - gen sprin - gen, die
Den lie - ben Gott lass' ich nur wal - ten, der

schickt er in die wei - te Welt, dem will er sei - ne Wun - der
Ler - chen schwir - ren hoch vor Lust. Wie sollt' ich nicht mit ih - nen
Bäch - lein, Ler - chen, Wald und Feld und Erd' und Him - mel will er -

wei - sen in Berg und Tal und Strom und Feld.
sin - gen aus vol - ler Kehl' und fri - scher Brust.
hal - ten, hat auch mein' Sach' aufs best' be - stellt.

11

Diphthongs

Especially in singing diction, the first vowel of a diphthong receives more stress and is longer in duration than the second vowel, which is called a diphthongal off-glide. This diphthongal off-glide is indicated with a diacritic called a subscript arch,[1] which indicates that the vowel is nonsyllabic: [aǫ, aę, ɔǫ].[2]

SECTION 1: *au*

[aǫ]

The German diphthong [aǫ], as in *Haus* [haǫs], is similar to the English diphthong [aʊ], as in *house* [haʊs]. The English diphthong begins with the front vowel [a] and ends with an open [ʊ].

In Chapter 9 we pointed out that, in German, the symbol [a] is now used to indicate a central vowel, thus farther back than the English vowel. The German diphthong begins with this more central [a] and ends with a short closed [o].[3]

---

[1]Siebs states that this "more weakly articulated" part of the diphthong is regularly indicated with a diacritic, but then goes on to say that one will not be used in the transcriptions of German diphthongs in *Deutsche Aussprache* (pp. 50–51).

[2]In order to reflect the distinct nature of these diphthongs in German, Siebs defends using symbols which depart from the recommendations of the IPA (p. 50). The current symbols given by the IPA for these German diphthongs is: [aʊ, aɪ, ɔɪ]

[3]Siebs describes this diphthong as a "progression from a (somewhat darker) short [ɑ] to a very short closed [o]" (p. 81). Other transcriptions found in standard references include: [ɑo, ao, aɤ, aṵ, aʊ, aǫ, aʊ, aːo, aːʊ, aːʊ, ãõ]

Exercise 11.1

Pronounce the following words:

1. Maus, Laus, Faust, lauschen, hinauslaufen
2. rauschen, Pause, Schmaus, austauschen, auflegen

Excerpt

Es rauschen die Wipfel und schauern,	Here the treetops rustle and shudder
Als machten zu dieser Stund'	as though, at this hour,
Um die halbversunkenen Mauern	through the half-sunken walls
Die alten Götter die Rund'.	the old gods were making their rounds.

Schöne Fremde
Eichendorff/Schumann

SECTION 2: *ei*

(Alternate, usually older, spellings of this diphthong include *ai*, *ey*, *ay*, as in: *Mai, Meyer, Bayern.*)

[ae̯]

The sound of German *ei*, as in *mein* [mae̯n] "my," is similar to the English diphthong [aɪ] in *mine* [maɪn]. The English diphthong begins with the front vowel [a] and ends with an open [ɪ]. The German diphthong begins with the more central German [a] and ends with a short closed [e]. Note, however, that many singers tend to open the second vowel somewhat, more in the direction of [ɛ].[4]

The singer should be exceptionally careful not to confuse *ei* with *ie*. The two are never pronounced the same. Even if they occur in different forms of the same verb, *ei* is pronounced [ae̯] and *ie* is pronounced [iː], as in *ihr schreibt* [ʃrae̯pt] "you write," *ihr schriebt* [ʃriːpt] "you wrote."

---

[4]Other transcriptions found in standard references include: [ɑe, aɪ̯, a̯i, ae̯, ae, aɪ, aːe, aːi, aːɪ, a͡e]

Exercise 11.2   Pronounce the following words:

1. Eiche, beichten, Geige, aussteigen, Kaiser
2. Heide, Waise, Weise, Wiese, Hain, Bay'reuth
3. gleich, Maid, Freiheit, Saite, Seite, Kleinod
4. schreien, schrieen, gedeihen, gediehen, feiern
5. Melodie, Melodien, Melodei, Melodeien

Excerpts   1.

Und ich geh' mit einer, die mich lieb hat,	And I walk with one who loves me,
ruhigen Gemütes in die Kühle	(my) spirit calm, into the coolness
dieses weißen Hauses, in den Frieden,	of this white house, into the peace
der voll Schönheit wartet, daß wir kommen.	which, full of beauty, waits for us to come.

Freundliche Vision
Bierbaum/Strauß

2.

Heiß mich nicht reden, heiß mich schweigen,	Bid me not to speak, bid me be silent,
Denn mein Geheimnis ist mir Pflicht;	for my secret is my duty;
Ich möchte dir mein ganzes Innre zeigen,	I long to show you my whole self,
Allein das Schicksal will es nicht.	but fate will not permit it.

Mignon II
Goethe/Wolf

Recording   Practice reading the text of the following song. Then record it without pausing.

Die Rose, die Lilie, die Taube, die Sonne,	The rose, the lily, the dove, the sun,
Die liebt' ich einst alle in Liebeswonne.	I loved them all once in love's ecstasy.
Ich lieb' sie nicht mehr, ich liebe alleine	I love them no more, I love only
Die Kleine, die Feine, die Reine, die Eine;	the small (one), the refined (one), the pure (one)— the One;
Sie selber, aller Liebe Wonne,	she herself, delight of all love,
Ist Rose und Lilie und Taube und Sonne.	is rose and lily and dove and sun.

Dichterliebe
Heine/R. Schumann

Song   Sing the following song, paying close attention to the pronunciation of *ei*.

Ihr kleinen Vögelein,	You little birds,
ihr Waldergötzerlein,	you little forest-delights,
ihr süßen Sängerlein,	you sweet little singers,
stimmt alle mit mir ein!	all sing along with me!
Ich will den Herren preisen	I want to praise the Lord
mit meinen Liebesweisen.	with my songs of love.
Ich will von Herzensgrund	I want from the bottom of my heart
ihm auftun meinen Mund!	to sing out for Him.
Spitzt eure Schnäbelein,	Sharpen your little beaks,
zwingt eure Stimmelein	direct your little voices,
und fangt an, groß und klein,	and begin, large and small,
aufs lieblichste zu schrein.	in the sweetest way to shout.
Ich will durch euer Singen	I want, through your singing,
mich zu dem Schöpfer schwingen.	to wing my way to the Creator.
Ich will durch euer'n Ton	I want, through your sound,
hinan zu Gottes Sohn.	(to rise) upward to God's son.
Drum stimmet mit mir ein,	So sing along with me,
ihr süßen Schreierlein,	you sweet little squawkers,
ihr kleinen Pfeiferlein,	you tiny little pipers,
ihr Wundersängerlein:	you wondrous little singers:
Gott Lob ist mein Erschallen,	"Praise God!" is my cry,
Gott Lob sei eu'r Erhallen.	"Praise God!" be your echo.
Gott Lob ist mein Gesang,	"Praise God!" is my song,
Gott Lob sei euer Klang,	may "Praise God!" be yours.

Ihr kleinen Vögelein

Ihr klei - nen_ Vö - ge - lein, ihr Wald - er - göt - zer - lein, ihr sü - ßen
Spitzt eu - re_ Schnä - be - lein, zwingt eu - re Stim - me - lein und fangt als_
Er ziert euch Feld und Wald so schön und man - nig - falt. Er kleid't euch
Drum stim - met_ mit mir ein, ihr sü - ßen Schrei - er - lein ihr klei - nen

Sän - ger - lein, stimmt al - le mit mir_ ein! Ich
groß und_ klein, aufs lieb - lich - ste zu_ schrein. Ich
jung und_ alt, mit Fe - dern wohl ge - stalt. Er
Pfei - fer - lein, ihr Wun - der - sän - ger - lein: Gott

will den Her - ren prei - sen mit mei - nen Lie - bes - wei - sen. Ich will von
will durch eu - er Sin - gen mich zu dem Schöp - fer schwin - gen. Ich will durch
schafft euch küh - le Sit - ze für Un - fall und für Hit - ze. Er gibt euch
Lob ist mein Er - schal - len, Gott Lob sei eu'r Er - hal - len. Gott Lob ist

Her - zens - grund ihm auf - tun   mei - nen   Mund!
eu - ern Ton hin - an   zu   Got - tes   Sohn.
Speis   und Trank und Mut   zum Lust - ge - sang.
mein Ge - sang,   Gott Lob   sei   eu - er   Klang.

SECTION 3: *eu, äu*

Just as the diphthongs *ei* and *au* are pronounced differently from their English equivalents, the German diphthong [ɔø], as in *Fäuste* ['fɔøstə] "fists," is more closed and more rounded than the English diphthong [ɔɪ] in *foist* [fɔɪst]. Both *eu* and *äu* are pronounced [ɔø]: *Leute* ['lɔøtə] "people," *läute* ['lɔøtə] "ring."[5]

Occasionally, *e* and *u* appear together as parts of two different elements, as in *beurteilen* "judge"; in such a case, they are of course pronounced separately: [bə'ʊrˌtae̯lən].

The singer is cautioned particularly about noting the distinction between the vowels in related words containing *au* and *äu*, such as *Haus* [haɔs] "house," *Häuser* ['hɔøzɐ] "houses."

Exercise 11.3

Contrast *au* and *äu* in the following pairs of related words:

1. lauft   läuft

2. Strauß   Sträuße

3. rauben   Räuber

4. Maus   Mäuse

---

[5]Other transcriptions found in standard references include: [ɔø, ɔy, ɔɪ, ɔœ, ɔʏ, ɔːʏ, oːi, ɔːɪ, ɔ̃ø]

Exercise 11.4

Pronounce the following words:

1. Täufer, Teufel, feucht, leuchten, Säule

2. Bräutigam, Braut, Frau, Fräulein, zeugen

3. liebäugeln, Efeu, beugen, beunruhigen, Unkraut

4. Streuselkuchen, treuster, Feuer, Löwenbräu

Exercise 11.5

Read the following transcription aloud:

[ʃoː ˈkyːlɐ valt, voː ˈraʊʃəst duː,
ⁱn deːm maɛn ˈliːpçən geːt?
ʃoː ˈviːdɐˌhal, voː laʊʃəst duː,
deːɐ gɛrn maɛn liːt fɛɐˈʃteːt?
ⁱm ˈhɛrtsən tiːf daː raʊʃt deːɐ valt,
ⁱn deːm maɛn ˈliːpçən geːt,
ⁱn ˈʃmɛrtsən ʃliːf deːɐ ˈvidɐˌhal,
diː ˈliːdɐ zɪnt fɛɐˈveːt]

Excerpts   1.

Streuet ihm, Schwestern,	Scatter for him, sisters,
Streuet ihm Blumen,	scatter for him flowers,
Bringet ihm knospende Rosen dar.	present to him budding roses;
Aber euch, Schwestern,	But you, sisters,
Grüß' ich mit Wehmut,	I bid farewell wistfully,
Freudig scheidend aus eurer Schar.	joyfully departing from your group.

Frauenliebe und -leben
Chamisso/R. Schumann

2.

Fleuch, Nachtigall, in grüne Finsternisse,	Flee, nightingale, into green darkness,
Ins Haingesträuch,	into the bushes of the grove,
Und spend' im Nest der treuen Gattin Küsse;	and in the nest shower your faithful wife with kisses;
Entfleuch, entfleuch!	fly away, fly away!

An die Nachtigall
Hölty/Brahms

3.

Sitz nieder, hier dämmert's geheimnisvoll Unter den Lindenbäumen, Die Nachtigall uns zu Häupten soll Von unsren Küssen träumen...	Sit down, here dusk is gathering mysteriously under the linden trees, The nightingale above our heads shall dream of our kisses...

Ständchen
Schack/Strauß

 4.

Die schönen weißen Wolken ziehn dahin Durchs tiefe Blau, wie schöne stille Träume, Mir ist, als ob ich längst gestorben bin Und ziehe selig mit durch ew'ge Räume.	The lovely white clouds drift along through (the) deep blue like lovely quiet dreams, I feel as though I died long ago and drift blissfully with (them) through eternal space.

Feldeinsamkeit
Allmers/Brahms

Song Sing the following song, paying special attention to the words containing *eu* and *äu*.

Das Leben bringt groß' Freud', Es wissen's alle Leut'. Weiß mir ein schönes Schätzelein Mit zwei schwarzbraunen Äugelein, Die mir mein Herz erfreut.	Life brings great joy, everyone knows that! I'm thinking of a lovely sweetheart with two dark brown eyes who gladdens my heart.
Ein Brieflein schrieb sie mir, Ich sollt' treu bleiben ihr. Drauf schickt' ich ihr ein Sträußelein, Schön Rosmarin und Nägelein, Sie soll mein eigen sein.	A little note she wrote me: I should remain true to her. Then I sent her a little bouquet, lovely rosemary and little carnations: She shall be my own.
Mein eigen soll sie sein, Keinem andern mehr als mein. So leben wir in Freud' und Leid, Bis Gott, der Herr, auseinander scheid't. Dann ade, mein Schatz, ade!	My own shall she be, no one else's, only mine. Then we'll live in joy and sorrow until the Lord God shall make us part. Then farewell, my sweet, farewell!

Das Lieben bringt groß' Freud'

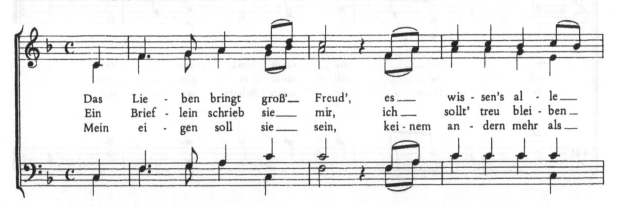

Das   Lie - ben bringt groß'__ Freud',   es__   wis - sen's al - le__
Ein   Brief - lein schrieb sie__ mir,   ich__   sollt' treu blei - ben__
Mein   ei - gen soll sie__ sein,   kei - nem an - dern mehr als

Leut'.   Weiß__   mir ein schö - nes   Schät - ze - lein   mit__
ihr.   Drauf__ schickt' ich ihr ein   Sträu - ße - lein,   schön__
mein.   So__   le - ben wir in   Freud'__ und__ Leid,   bis__

zwei schwarz - brau - nen__   Äu - ge - lein,   die__   mir,   die__
Ros - ma - rin,__ und__   Nä - ge - lein,   sie__   soll,   sie__
Gott, der Herr, aus - ein - an - der - scheid't. Dann a - de,   dann a -

mir,   die____   mir   mein Herz   er -   freut.
soll,   sie____   soll   mein ei - gen____   sein.
de!   Dann a - de,   mein Schatz, a -   de!

SECTION 4:
OTHER VOWEL
COMBINATIONS

In vowel combinations other than those specifically discussed, each member will be pronounced separately, as in *Poet* [po'eːt], *aktuell* [aktu'ɛl].

Exercise 11.6   Pronounce the following:

1. Krea'tur, Dia'mant, Du'ell, ide'al
2. säen, böig, Poe'sie

12

The Sounds of *l*; the Sounds of *r* (Conclusion)

SECTION 1: *l*, *ll*

[l] (lower-case L)

In the English word *fell,* the sound [l] is articulated with the tongue cupped downward in the middle and the tip resting high up on the alveolar ridge. In the German word *Fell,* the sound [l] (no difference in transcription) is articulated with the tongue nearly flat and the tip resting very low on the alveolar ridge, almost against the upper teeth. We refer to this articulation of *l* as the "light" *l* (also called "clear" *l* or "bright" *l*).

Exercise 12.1 Contrast the pronunciation of *l* in the following pairs:

English	German
fell	Fell
Helen	hellen
fleck	Fleck
lope	Lob

173

ll

One Element [l]

In general, *ll* is pronounced the same as *l*, as in fällen ['fɛlən] "to fell."[1]

Two Elements [l̲l̲]

When *ll* represents parts of two elements, it is markedly lengthened and divided between notes, as in *fühllos* "unfeeling." This lengthening may be indicated with a tie bar: ['fyːl̡loːs].

Exercise 12.2

Pronounce the following words:

1. Ball, Lampe, schlau, Schulter, fällen
2. blassen, ablassen, allmächtig, all'liebend, Balsam
3. Lieder, Walter, geblichen, vergeblichen, behaglich
4. Milch, Dolch, solch, gelb, Geld, Klang, glich, Kla'vier
5. wohllautender, tadellos, heillos, bewilligen, vielleicht

Songs

Sing the following songs, concentrating on the special articulation of German *l*.

Mein Herz ist voll Lieder,	My heart is full of songs,
Die Seele voll Sang;	my soul full of singing;
Was ich auch spielte	whatever I'd perform
Ist Frohsinn, ist Sang;	is merriness, is singing;
Durch Felder und Auen	through fields and river meadows
Nur eine Melodei:	just one melody:
Mein Schatz ist ein Spielmann,	My sweetheart is a minstrel,
Tandaradei!	(Tra la la!)
Und käme mein Schatz	And (if) my sweetheart came
Mit mir in den Wald,	with me into the forest,
Die Vöglein alle,	the little birds all,
Die schwiegen gar bald,	they would fall silent soon
Und lauschten auf seine	and would listen to his
So frohen Melodei'n:	so-cheerful melodies:
Mein Schatz ist ein Spielmann,	My sweetheart is a minstrel,
Tandaradei!	(Tra la la!)

[1]Some singers may extend the consonant, depending on expressive intention.

Mein Herz ist voll Lieder

Mein   Herz   ist   voll   Lie - der,   die   See - le   voll
Und   kä - me   mein   Schatz   mit   mir   in   den

Sang;   was   ich   auch   spiel - te   ist   Froh - sinn, ist   Sang;   durch
Wald,   die   Vög - lein   al - le,   die   schwie - gen gar   bald,   und

Fel - der   und   Au - en   nur   ei - ne   Me - lo - dei: Mein
lausch - ten   auf   sei - ne   so   fro - hen   Me - lo - dei'n: Mein

Schatz   ist   ein   Spiel - mann,   tan - da - ra - dei,   mein
Schatz   ist   ein   Spiel - mann,   tan - da - ra - dei,   mein

Schatz ist ein Spiel - mann, tan - da - ra - dei.
Schatz ist ein Spiel - mann, tan - da - ra - dei.

Auf der Lüneburger Heide,	Upon the Lüneburg heath
In dem wunderschönen Land,	in the wondrously beautiful countryside,
Ging ich auf und ging ich unter,	I wandered up and I wandered down,
Allerlei am Weg ich fand.	lots of things along the way I found.
Valeri, valera und juchheirassa,	Valeri, valera, and juchheirassa (rejoicing),
Bester Schatz, denn du weißt es,	dearest love, because you know it,
Weißt es ja.	yes, you know it!
Brüder, lasst die Gläser klingen,	Brothers, let our glasses ring,
Denn der Muskateller Wein	for the muscatel wine
Wird vom langen Stehen sauer,	becomes sour from standing too long,
Ausgetrunken muss er sein!	we must drink it up!
(Refrain)	(Refrain)
Und die Hunde und die bellen,	And the dogs and they bark,
Und die Büchse und die knallt,	and the rifle and it goes bang,
Rote Hirsche woll'n wir jagen	red deer we want to hunt
In dem grünen, grünen Wald.	in the green, green forest.
(Refrain)	(Refrain)

Auf der Lüneburger Heide

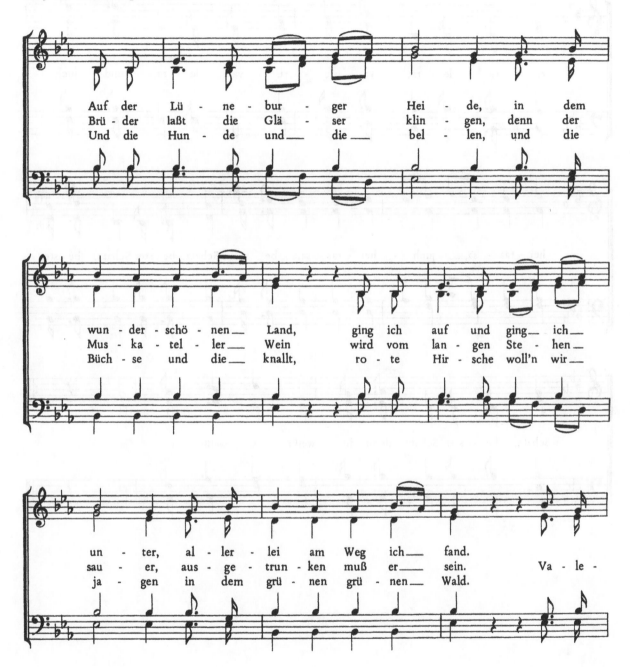

Auf der Lü - ne - bur - ger Hei - de, in dem
Brü - der laßt die Glä - ser klin - gen, denn der
Und die Hun - de und die bel - len, und die

wun - der - schö - nen Land, ging ich auf und ging ich
Mus - ka - tel - ler Wein wird vom lan - gen Ste - hen
Büch - se und die knallt, ro - te Hir - sche woll'n wir

un - ter, al - ler - lei am Weg ich fand.
sau - er, aus - ge - trun - ken muß er sein. Va - le -
ja - gen in dem grü - nen grü - nen Wald.

SECTION 2: *r, rr* (CONCLUSION)

Postvocalic *r* [ɐ̯]

In Chapter 5, we advised the singer to adopt the articulation [ɐ̯], [ɐ]—a vowel-like sound used for *r* in final position in certain monosyllables and prefixes and for the final syllable *-er*, but to use the single-tap trill [ɾ] for *r* in other positions. It may have become apparent that no singer strictly adheres to this differentiation. However, it has probably also become apparent that no singer uses *only* the trill. The English-speaking singer, in part influenced by Italian diction, in part for simplicity's sake, tends to use the trill for all *r*s. This results in an unduly severe sound, especially in the art song. By offering simplified rules for the use of [ɾ] and [ɐ̯], [ɐ], we hoped to help the singer develop confidence in the use of the vocalic *r* in singing German.

Now let us review and expand the guidelines for the use of [ɾ] and [ɐ̯], [ɐ]. Although [ɐ̯] *may* be used for any final or preconsonantal *r*, it occurs most frequently in the following words and elements:

1.	the article	*der* [deːɐ̯]	"the"
2.	the pronouns	*mir* [miːɐ̯]	"me"
		dir [diːɐ̯]	"you"
		er [eːɐ̯]	"he"
		ihr [iːɐ̯]	"her," "you"
		wir [viːɐ̯]	"we"
		wer [veːɐ̯]	"who"
3.	the prepositions	*für* [fyːɐ̯]	"for"
		vor [voːɐ̯]	"before"
4.	the prefixes	*her-* [heːɐ̯] (stressed), [heɐ̯] (unstressed)	
		er- [ɛɐ̯]	
		ver- [fɛɐ̯]	
		zer- [tsɛɐ̯]	

5. After a long vowel

After a long vowel, *r* is generally pronounced [ɐ] when it appears in final position or before a consonant.

Final: Meer [meːɐ] "sea," sehr [zeːɐ] "very," Bier [biːɐ] "beer," hier [hiːɐ] "here," vier [fiːɐ] "four," Haar [haːɐ] "hair," Flur [fluːɐ] "meadow," Uhr [uːɐ] "clock," etc.

Before a consonant: werden [ˈveːɐdən] "become," Erde [ˈeːɐdə] "earth," Herd [heːɐt] "hearth," zart [tsaːɐt] "gentle," etc.

Unstressed -*er* [ɐ]

The final syllable -*er* is usually pronounced [ɐ] when it is unstressed and is final in an element, or final before a consonant, as in *aber* [ˈaːbɐ] "but," *besser* [ˈbɛsɐ] "better," *Kindergarten* [ˈkɪndɐˌɡaʁtən], *mildert* [ˈmɪldɐt] "softens," and *hundert* [ˈhʊndɐt] "hundred."

Other Postvocalic *r* [ɾ]

Otherwise, the pronunciation of *r* is the one-tap trill [ɾ]. The singer is urged to use [ɾ] when it appears before a consonant after a stressed short vowel, as in *warten* [ˈvaɾtən] "wait," *fertig* [ˈfɛɾtɪç] "finished."

The choice of articulation for *r* can be of considerable expressive importance in the interpretation of a song. Many singers use the trill almost exclusively, especially for baroque music and Wagner. Others prefer to use the trill more sparingly, thereby achieving a softer quality. It is recommended that beginning singers adopt the latter approach. This allows for more effective use of the one-tap trill [ɾ]—or the longer trill [r]—for emphasis and force.

rr

One Element

In one element, *rr* is usually pronounced [ɾ], as in *sperren* [ˈʃpɛɾən] "lock," *dürr* [dʏɾ] "dry," *irrt* [ɪɾt] "errs."

Two Elements

When *rr* represents parts of two elements, it is usually pronounced [ɐr], as in *Vorrede* [ˈfoːɐˌreːdə] "introduction," *erraten* [ɛɐˈraːtən] "guess."

Some singers use an extended trill for *rr* in simple words and compounds, as well as for *r* in blends, such as *fr* and *tr*. This articulation should be avoided by the beginner.

Exercise 12.3   Pronounce the following words:

1. Torheit, ereilt, beerben, dankerfüllten
2. vereint, wieder'holt, Verräter, ehrerbietig, arglos
3. Meisterehre, Meisterregeln, erreicht, surren
4. feuerrot, herrlich, herreiten, Irrtum, Winterreise
5. daran, fort'an, hervorrufen, herüberreiten

Exercise 12.4   Transcribe the above words into the IPA.

Songs   Practice the different articulations of *r* by singing the following song.

Es, es, es und es,
Es ist ein harter Schluss,
Weil, weil, weil und weil,
Weil ich aus Frankfurt muss.
Drum schlag' ich Frankfurt aus dem Sinn
Und wende mich, Gott weiß wohin.
Ich will mein Glück probieren,
Marschieren!

Er, er, er und er,
Herr Meister leb' er wohl!
(Repeat)
Ich sag's ihm grad' frei ins Gesicht,
Seine Arbeit, die gefällt mir nicht.
Ich will mein Glück probieren,
Marschieren!

Sie, sie, sie und sie,
Frau Meist'rin leb' sie wohl!
(Repeat)
Ich sag's ihr grad' frei ins Gesicht,
Ihr Speck und Kraut, das schmeckt mir nicht.
Ich will mein Glück probieren,
Marschieren!

Ihr, ihr, ihr und ihr,
Ihr Jungfern lebet wohl!
(Repeat)
Ich wünsch' euch jetzt zu guter Letzt
Einen andern, der mein' Stell' ersetzt.
Ich will mein Glück probieren,
Marschieren!

It, it, it, and it,
it's a tough conclusion,
because, because, because and because
because I must (get) out of Frankfurt.
So I'll put Frankfurt out of my mind
and head God knows where.
I want to try my luck
(and) march away!

He, he, he, and he,
my master, may he fare well!
(Repeat)
I'll tell him right to his face:
His work, I don't like it.
I want to try my luck
and march away!

She, she, she, and she,
may the master's wife fare well!
(Repeat)
I'll tell her right to her face:
Her bacon and sauerkraut I can't stand!
I want to try my luck
and march away!

You, you, you and you,
you young ladies, fare well!
(Repeat)
I wish you now, last of all,
another guy who'll take my place.
I want to try my luck
and march away!

Es, es, es und es

□ 13 □

The Sounds of *h*, *j*

SECTION 1: *h*

Silent[1]

In general, *h* is not pronounced after a vowel, unless it begins an element. Specifically, postvocalic *h* is silent: (1) at the end of a word or element, as in *Floh* [floː] "flea," *Gehrock* [ˈgeːˌrɔk] "coat"; (2) before a consonant, as in *steht* [ʃteːt] "stands"; and (3) intervocalically in one element, as in *gehen* [ˈgeːən] "go."[2]

[h] (lower-case H)

The voiceless glottal fricative [h] is used for *h* at the beginning of a word or element, as in *Hand* [hant] "hand," *gehören* [gəˈhøːrən] "belong." It is sometimes difficult for the novice to determine whether *h* begins an element: for example, *froher* "merry" is made up of *froh* + *er* and is pronounced [ˈfroːɐ], whereas *woher* is made up of *wo* + *her* and is pronounced [voˈheːɐ]. The following words, which can prove troublesome, should be learned:

---

[1]See Chapter 14 for a discussion of *th*.

[2]Occasionally singers pronounce the *h* in a slow passage in a word like *gehen* [ˈgeːhən]. This practice should be avoided; but the singer should also be careful not to confuse this situation with that in which *h* begins a new element (see next paragraph).

185

behende [bə'hɛndə]	"quick"
woher [vo'heːɐ̯]	"whence"
daher [da'heːɐ̯, 'daːˌheːɐ̯]	"therefore, from there"
dahin [da'hɪn, 'daːˌhɪn]	"thither, (to) there"

Exercise 13.1

Pronounce the following words, observing the rules for pronunciation of *h:*

1. ruhen, ehe, eher, fliehen, Halle, Kindheit
2. hoher, wo'her, jähes, bis'her, ein'her, wo'hin
3. geheim, Gehege, gehende, bebende, Freiheit
4. Friedhof, gehorchen, Höhe, höhere, Hoheit,
5. wieder'holt, behutsam, ab'handen, all'hier
6. Gotteshaus, Drehorgel, Strohhalm, unbarmherzig

Excerpts   1.

Schon krähen die Hähne, Und nah ist der Ort. .... Wohl seh' ich, Herrin, die Kraft dir schwinden ...	Already the cocks are crowing, and the town is near. .... I see well, (my) lady, (how) your strength wanes—

Nun wandre, Maria
Geibel, Heyse/Wolf

2.

Fort in die Freiheit! Dahin gehör' ich, Da, wo ich Meister im Haus!	Forward into freedom! There I belong, there, where I am master of my house.

Die Meistersinger
Wagner

SECTION 2: *j*

[j] (lower-case J)

In most words, *j* is pronounced as the voiced palatal fricative (or glide) [j], as in *Jammer* ['jamɐ] "plaint," *bejahen* [bə'jaːən] "affirm," *Major* [ma'joːɐ̯] "major," *Kajak* ['kaːjak] "kayak."

[ʒ] (ezh *or* tailed Z)

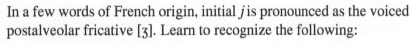

In a few words of French origin, initial *j* is pronounced as the voiced postalveolar fricative [ʒ]. Learn to recognize the following:

Jalousie [ʒalu'ziː]

Jackett [ʒa'kɛt]

Jargon [ʒaɐ'gõː]

Journal [ʒʊɐ'naːl]

Exercise 13.2

Pronounce the following words:

1. ja, jetzt, jodeln, Majes'tät, Januar, Jugend
2. Jünger, Journa'list, gejagt, Jäger, Jas'min, gejubelt

14

The Sounds of *z, p, t, k, x, qu*

SECTION 1: *z, zz, tz*

z [ts]

The letter *z* is pronounced [ts] in all positions: *Zeit* [tsaɛt] "time," *bezahlen* [bəˈtsaːlən] "pay," *tanzen* [ˈtantsən] "dance," *Kreuz* [krɔøts] "cross."

zz [ts]

In words of Italian origin, *zz* is pronounced [ts]: *Skizze* [ˈskɪtsə] "sketch," *Pizza* "pizza" [ˈpɪtsa].

tz

One Element [ts]

When it occurs within one element, *tz* is pronounced the same as *z*: *setzen* [ˈzɛtsən] "set," *Schatz* [ʃats] "treasure."

Two Elements [t͡ts]

When *t* belongs to one element and *z* to the next, the *t* is extended, as in *entzücken* "to charm," and the extended consonant may be represented with a tie bar: [ɛnt͡tsʏkən].

Exercise 14.1   Pronounce the following words:

1. Platz, Nutzen, trotz, jetzt, Speze'rei, gezeigt
2. Zimmer, Frauenzimmer, Zoo, Zürich, zogst
3. verzichten, Wurzel, stürzt, jauchzen, spa'zieren
4. Walzer, Lenz, Holz, kreuzigten, Geächze, zu'erst
5. Erzengel, erziehen, erzürnt, herzlos, herziehen
6. zitternd, Zephyr, zu'sammen, herzerschütternd

Excerpts   1.

Und nichts zu forschen, nichts zu spähn,	And to seek nothing, to watch for nothing,
Und nur zu träumen leicht und lind,	and just to dream, gently and sweetly,
Der Zeiten Wandel nicht zu sehn,	not to see the changing of the times,
Zum zweiten Mal ein Kind!	for the second time (to be) a child!

0 wüsst' ich doch den Weg zurück
Groth/Brahms

2.

Da tanzt wohl den Hochzeitsreigen	There dancing her wedding dance (is) surely
Die Herzallerliebste mein.	my dearest beloved.

Das ist ein Flöten und Geigen
Heine/Schumann

Recordings

Practice reading the text of the following song; then record it without pausing.

Es grünet ein Nussbaum vor dem Haus,	A nut tree grows green before the house;
Duftig,	fragrantly,
Luftig	airily,
Breitet er blättrig die Äste aus.	it spreads its leafy branches wide.
Viel liebliche Blüten stehen dran;	Many lovely blossoms are on them,
Linde	gentle
Winde	winds
Kommen, sie herzlich zu umfahn.	come to encircle them warmly.
Es flüstern je zwei zu zwei gepaart,	They whisper, paired two by two,
Neigend,	leaning,
Beugend	bending
Zierlich zum Kusse die Häuptchen zart.	their delicate little heads gracefully for a kiss.
Sie flüstern von einem Mägdlein, das	They whisper about a girl who
Dächte	would think
Nächte	(for) nights
Tagelang, wusste, ach, selber nicht was.	(and) days, (but) knew not herself, alas, (of) what!
Sie flüstern, wer mag verstehn so gar	They whisper—who can understand so
Leise	soft
Weise?	(a) strain?
Flüstern von Bräut'gam und nächstem Jahr.	(They) whisper about (a) bridegroom and next year.
Das Mägdlein horchet, es rauscht im Baum;	The girl listens, there's rustling in the tree;
Sehnend,	longing,
Wähnend	thinking,
Sinkt es lächelnd in Schlaf und Traum.	she slips smiling into sleep and dream.

Der Nussbaum
Mosen/Schumann

Song   Sing the following song, concentrating on the pronunciation of *z*.

Morgen muss ich fort von hier	Tomorrow I must (go) away from here
Und muss Abschied nehmen;	and must take (my) leave;
O du allerschönste Zier,	oh, you loveliest gem,
Scheiden, das bringt Grämen.	parting—that brings grief.
Da ich dich so treu geliebt	Since I've loved you so faithfully,
Über alle Maßen,	beyond all measure,
Soll ich dich verlassen?	shall I leave you?
Wenn zwei gute Freunde sind,	When two are good friends,
Die einander kennen,	who know one another,
Sonn' und Mond bewegen sich,	sun and moon (would sooner) move
Ehe sie sich trennen.	before the two separate.
Noch viel größer ist der Schmerz,	Yet even greater is the pain
Wenn ein treu verliebtes Herz	when a faithful heart in love
In die Fremde ziehet.	moves far away.
Küsset dir ein Lüftelein	(If) a little breeze kisses
Wangen oder Hände,	your cheeks or hands,
Denke, dass es Seufzer sind,	think of it as sighs
Die ich zu dir sende;	that I send to you;
Tausend schick' ich täglich aus,	a thousand (will) I send out daily,
Die da wehen um dein Haus,	which (will) waft around your house,
Weil ich dein gedenke.	because I am thinking of you.

Morgen muß ich fort

Mor - gen muß ich fort von hier und muß Ab - schied
Wenn zwei gu - te Freun - de sind, die ein - an - der
Küs - set dir ein Lüf - te - lein Wan - gen o - der

neh - men; o du al - ler - schön - ste Zier, Schei - den, das____ bringt
ken - nen, Sonn' und Mond be - we - gen sich, e - he sie____ sich
Hän - de, den - ke, daß es Seuf - zer sind, die ich zu____ dir

Grä - men. Da ich dich so treu ge - liebt
tren - nen. Noch viel grö - ßer ist der Schmerz,
sen - de; tau - send schick' ich täg - lich aus,

ü	-	ber	al	-	le	Ma	-	ßen,	soll	ich	dich	ver -
wenn	ein	treu	ver	-	lieb	-	tes	Herz	in	die	Frem	- de
die	da	we	-	hen	um	dein	Haus,	weil	ich	dein	ge -

las	-	sen,___	soll	ich___	dich	ver	las	-	sen.
zie	-	het,___	in	die___	Frem	- de	zie	-	het.
den	-	ke,___	weil	ich___	dein	ge	-	den	-	ke.

SECTION 2: *p,*
pp, pf, ps, ph

p [p] (lower-case P)

As in English, *p* represents the voiceless bilabial stop [p], as in *Pein* [paɛn] "pain," *geprahlt* [gəˈpraːlt] "boasted."

pp [p]

pp is usually pronounced the same as *p*, as in *Lippe* [ˈlɪpə] "lip," *Suppe* [ˈzʊpə] "soup," *schnappt* [ʃnapt] "snaps."[1]

---
[1]Some singers may extend the consonant, depending on expressive intention.

pf [pf]

The combination *pf* always represents the affricate [pf]. When it occurs at the beginning of a word or element, as in *Pfad* [pfaːt] "path," *gepfiffen* [gəˈpfɪfən] "whistled," it is launched as a unit on the same note. If it occurs intervocalically in a noncompound word such as *Apfel* [ˈapfəl] "apple," the [p] is usually begun on one beat and released as [f] on the next. The singer must be careful to sound the [p] in this combination.

Exercise 14.2   Pronounce:

1. Pfeife, Pferd, Pflanze
2. tapfer, Gipfel, klopfen

ps [ps]

The combination *ps* is always pronounced [ps], even at the beginning of a word, as in *Psalm* [psalm].

ph [f] (lower-case F)

The combination *ph* is normally pronounced [f], as in *Phrase* [ˈfraːzə].[2]

Exercise 14.3   Pronounce:

1. Palme, Treppe, Doppelgänger, Pinie, Puppe
2. Pfeil, Pflaume, Schnaps, Phantaˈsie, prächtig
3. Posten, Pfosten, Pfriem, verpflichten, schlüpfen
4. gepflückt, Psyche, Proˈphet, Phönix, Pappeln, Sphären

---

[2]With the new spelling rules of 1996, many words with *ph* may also be spelled with *f*, e.g. *Saxoˈfon, Choroeograˈfie.*

Excerpt   1.

Die Trommel gerühret, das Pfeifchen gespielt!	The drum beats, the fife plays!
Mein Liebster gewaffnet dem Haufen befiehlt,	My beloved, armed, commands the group;
Die Lanze hoch führet, die Leute regieret.	his lance held high, (he) leads the people.
Wie klopft mir das Herz! Wie wallt mir das Blut!	How my heart pounds! How my blood races!

Die Trommel gerühret
Goethe/Beethoven

2.

Mit Tritten, wie Tritte der Elfen so sacht,	With steps like steps of the elves so gentle,
Um über die Blumen zu hüpfen,	for skipping over the flowers,
Flieg leicht hinaus in die Mondscheinnacht,	fly lightly out into the moonlight-night,
Zu mir in den Garten zu schlüpfen.	to slip into the garden to me.

Ständchen
Schack/Strauß

3.

Flieg her zum Krippelein,	Fly over here to the manger,
Flieg her, gefiedert Schwesterlein,	fly over here, feathered little sister,
Blas an den feinen Psalterlein,	play on your fine psaltery,
Sing, Nachtigall, gar fein!	sing, nightingale, your finest!

Wach, Nachtigall, wach auf!
Folk Song

Song   Sing the following song, concentrating on the pronunciation of
p and its combinations.

Der Apfel ist nicht gleich am Baum.	The apple isn't immediately on the tree.
Da war erst lauter Blüte.	there were first many blossoms.
Da war erst lauter Blütenschaum,	There was first a froth of blossoms,
Da war erst lauter Frühlingstraum	there was first the dream of spring
Und lauter Lieb' und Güte.	and so much love and goodness.
Dann waren Blätter grün an grün	Then came leaves, green on green
Und grün an grün nur Blätter.	and green on green just leaves.
Die Amsel nach des Tages Müh'n,	The blackbird, after the day's travails,
Sie sang ihr Abendlied gar kühn,	it sang its evening song so boldly,
Und auch bei Regenwetter.	and even in rainy weather.
Der Herbst, der macht die Blätter steif,	The autumn, it makes the leaves brittle,
Der Sommer muss sich packen.	the summer must make way.
Hei, dass ich auf dem Finger pfeif':	Hey, I whistle through my fingers:
Da sind die ersten Äpfel reif,	Here the first apples are ripe
Und haben rote Backen.	and have red cheeks!
Und was bei Sonn' und Himmel war,	And what was once in sun and sky
Erquickt nun Mund und Magen,	now refreshes mouth and stomach,
Und macht die Augen hell und klar.	and makes one's eyes bright and clear.
So rundet sich das Apfeljahr	Thus rounds out the apple-year
Und mehr ist nicht zu sagen.	and there's nothing more to say.

Der Apfel ist nicht gleich am Baum

SECTION 3: *t, tt, th, tsch, ti*

t [t] (lower-case T)

As in English, *t* usually represents the voiceless alveolar stop [t], as in *Tal* [taːl] "valley," *beten* [ˈbeːtən] "pray."

tt

One Element [t]

When it occurs in one element, as in *Betten* [ˈbɛtən] "beds," *Fittich* [ˈfɪtɪç] "wing," *tt* is usually pronounced [t].[3]

Two Elements [t͡t]

When *tt* represents parts of two elements, as in *Bettag* "day of prayer," the pronunciation is extended, and the extended consonant may be represented with a tie bar: [ˈbeːt͡taːk].

th

One Element [t]

When *th* does not represent parts of different elements, it is pronounced [t] and treated as a single consonant for phonetic considerations. In modern German, *th* appears in only a few words that are not compounds, for example *Theater* [teˈaːtɐ] "theater," *Apotheke* [apoˈteːkə] "pharmacy."

The archaic spelling *th* for *t* occurs in many texts, as in *Rath* [raːt] (modern: *Rat)* "counsel," *Theil* [taɛl] (modern: *Teil)* "part."

Two Elements [th]

In a number of words, *th* represents parts of two elements in a compound. Since in this case the second element begins with *h*, it is pronounced, as in *Rathaus* [ˈraːtˌhaɔs] "town hall."

tsch [t͡ʃ]

The combination *tsch* represents the affricate [t͡ʃ] as in *Deutsch* [dɔ͜øt͡ʃ] "German."

---

[3]Some singers may extend the consonant, depending on expressive intention.

ti [tsị]

In a number of words of Latin origin, *ti* is pronounced [tsị] (recall that the symbol [ị] is nonsyllabic). The only members of this group that might be of interest to the singer are those containing the syllable *-tion*, as in *Nation* [naˈtsịoːn], *Aktion* [akˈtsịoːn]. When the syllable *-tion* is final, it will be stressed.

Exercise 14.4

A. Pronounce the following words, observing the rules for the pronunciation of *t* and its combinations (some of the spellings are archaic):

1. Tat, Atem, Schatten, Retter, Hüte, Hütte
2. Auktion, Thema, rotglühend, Theˈrese, dritte
3. enttäuschen, muthig, Thränen, dorthin, Guttat
4. entrauschen, welthellsichtig, Thor, Festtag, flattern
5. Blüthendampfe, Posthorn, Beethoven, plätschern
6. Wehmutsstrahlen, Götter, Hauptton, weitˈher, Walther
7. bereithalten, Bettag, Bretter, bitter, rutschen
8. Funktion, Gasthaus, Peitsche, getheilt, enthält
9. Gasthof, Nation, Wehmuthsthränen, Liebeston, Zither
10. Mythe, mythisch, gutherzig, mitreisen, Aˈpostel, Äsˈthetik
11. Äther, liebestrunken, trösten, Eˈlisabeth, Urtheil

B. Transcribe the words in A above into the IPA.

Excerpts

Read the following excerpts aloud:

1.

So war es mein Kuss,	So was it my kiss
Der welthellsichtig dich machte?	that made you see the world clearly?
Mein volles Liebesumfangen	The full breadth of my love
lässt dich dann Gottheit erlangen.	will then transport you to godliness.

Parsifal
Wagner

2.

Noch war kein Tag, wo du und ich Nicht theilten unsre Sorgen.	There was yet no day when you and I did not share our cares.
Auch waren sie für dich und mich Getheilt leicht zu ertragen; Du tröstetest im Kummer mich, Ich weint' in deine Klagen ...	And they were for you and me, shared, easy to bear; you comforted me in sorrow, I wept with your laments…

Ich liebe dich
Herossee/Beethoven

SECTION 4: *k, kn, ck, kk*

k [k] (lower-case K)

The letter *k* is always pronounced [k], as in *kaum* [kaʊm] "hardly," *krumm* [krʊm] "crooked," *beklagen* [bəˈklaːɡən] "lament."

kn [kn]

It is important to note that in the combination *kn* the *k* is pronounced, as in *Knabe* [ˈknaːbə] "lad," *geknüpft* [ɡəˈknʏpft] "knotted."

ck [k]

The combination *ck* is pronounced [k], as in *nicken* [ˈnɪkən] "nod," *steckt* [ʃtɛkt] "sticks." When a word must be divided at *ck* in a musical score, it is spelled *k-k: lok-ki-gen* = *lockigen* "curly."

kk

One Element [k]

The double consonant *kk* appears in only a few words that are not compounds. In these words, which are usually of foreign origin, *kk* is pronounced [k], for example, in *Akkord* [aˈkɔrt] "chord."

Two Elements [k͡k]   Usually, *kk* represents parts of two elements, often in the form *ckk*, so the pronunciation is extended, and the extended consonant may be represented with a tie bar, as in *Rückkehr* ['rʏk͡keːɐ̯] "return."

Exercise 14.5   A. Pronounce:

1. Kahn, Kinn, kühl, Kur, verkaufen
2. Bäcker, versteckte, froh'locken, Hecken, Backofen
3. eklig, Knopf, akku'rat, Schmuckkasten
4. Pauke, Onkel, Birke, Schurke, Schalk
5. Waldecke, entrückte, Droschke, glücklich, zu'rückkehren
6. Edikt, Kerker, kräftig, Knackwurst, klopft
7. knüpfen, geknallt, Knie, Knospe, verkniffen
8. gekleidet, Kümmel, Klee, geklebt, Häkchen

B. Transcribe the words in A above into the IPA.

Excerpts   1.

Knusper, knusper, Knäuschen,	Crunch, crunch, crunchy,
Wer knuspert mir am Häuschen.	who nibbles on my little house?

Hänsel und Gretel
Humperdinck

2.

Petrus, der nicht denkt zurück,	Petrus, who, not reflecting,
Seinen Gott verneinet,	denies his God,
Der doch auf ein'n ernsten Blick	who, however, upon a stern glance,
Bitterlichen weinet:	bitterly weeps:
Jesu, blicke mich auch an,	Jesus, look at me also
Wenn ich nicht will büßen;	when I won't repent,
Wenn ich Böses hab' gethan,	when I've done wrong,
Rühre mein Gewissen.	stir my conscience.

Jesu Leiden, Pein und Tod
Bach

SECTION 5: *x* [ks]

The letter *x* is pronounced [ks], as in *Hexe* ['hɛksə] "witch," *Nixe* ['nɪksə] "nymph."

SECTION 6: *qu* [kv]

The combination *qu* is pronounced [kv], as in *Quarz* [kvaːʁts] "quartz."

Exercise 14.6

Pronounce:

Qual

Quali'tät

qualmen

einquartieren

entquellen

Exercise 14.7

Read the following transcription aloud:

[|alˈnɛçtlɪç |ɪm ˈtraɵmə zeː |ɪç dɪç
|ʊnt zeːə dɪç ˈfrɔøntlɪç ˈɡryːsən
|ʊnt laɵt |aɵfˌvaɵnənt ʃtʏʁts |ɪç mɪç
tsuː ˈdaɵnən ˈzyːsən ˈfyːsən

duː ˈziːəst mɪç |an ˈveːˌmyːtɪklɪç
|ʊnt ˈʃʏtəlst das ˈblɔndə ˈkœpfçən
|aɵs ˈdaɵnən |aɵɡən ˈʃlaɵçən zɪç
diː ˈpɛʁlənˌtreːnənˌtrœpfçən

duː zaːkst miːʁ ˈhaɵmlɪç |aɵn ˈlaɵzəs vɔrt
|ʊnt ɡiːpst miːʁ den ʃtraɵs fɔn tsyˈprɛsən
|ɪç ˈvaxə |aɵf, |ʊnt deːʁ ʃtraɵs |ɪst fɔrt
|ʊnts vɔrt haːp |ɪç fɛʁˈgesən]

Excerpt   Read the following excerpt aloud:

Das heiße Sündenblut entquillt,	The hot blood of sin wells up,
ewig erneut aus des Sehnens Quelle.	eternally renewed from the wellspring of longing.

Parsifal
Wagner

Song   Sing the following song.

Hänsel und Gretel verliefen sich im Wald,	Hänsel and Gretel got lost in the forest,
Es war so finster und auch so grimmig kalt.	it was so dark and so dreadfully cold.
Sie kamen an ein Häuschen von Pfefferkuchen fein:	They came to a little house of fine gingerbread:
Wer mag der Herr wohl in diesem Häuschen sein?	Whoever might the master of this little house be?
Hu, hu, da schaut' eine alte Hexe raus!	Oh no, then an old witch peered out!
Lockte die Kinder ins Pfefferkuchenhaus.	(She) lured the children into the gingerbread house.
Sie stellte sich gar freundlich, o Hänsel, welche Not!	She acted so friendly—oh, Hänsel, what danger!
Ihn wollt' die braten im Ofen braun wie Brot.	She wanted to bake him in the oven, brown as bread!
Doch als die Hexe zum Ofen schaut' hinein,	But as the witch looked into the oven,
Ward sie gestoßen vom Hans und Gretelein.	she was shoved by Hans and Gretelein.
Die Hexe musste braten, die Kinder geh'n nach Haus.	The witch had to roast, the children go home.
Nun ist das Märchen von Hans und Gretel aus.	Now is the tale of Hans and Gretel done.

Hänsel und Gretel

15

The Sounds of *c* and *ch* (Conclusion)[1]

SECTION 1: *c*

The letter *c* rarely occurs before a vowel in modern German. It does, however, occur in archaic spellings, which are fairly common in song texts.

[ts]

Before a front vowel, *c* is pronounced [ts]: *Cäsar* ['tsɛːzaɾ] "Caesar," *cis* [tsɪs] "C-sharp," *ces* [tsɛs] "C-flat."[2]

[k]

Before a back vowel, *c* is pronounced [k]: *Café* [ka'feː], *Cousin* [ku'zɛ̃].

---

[1] See Chapter 14 for *ck*.
[2] In *Cello, Cembalo, c* is pronounced [tʃ].

207

SECTION 2: *ch* (CONCLUSION)

[x] (lower-case X)

In Chapter 5, it was pointed out that *ch* is regularly pronounced as the voiceless velar fricative [x] after *a, o, u,* and *au: Bach* [bax], *Bruch* [brʊx].

[ç] (C cedilla)

1. After all other vowels and after consonants, *ch* is pronounced as the voiceless palatal fricative [ç]. It is especially important to be aware of this distinction in related forms with and without umlaut: *Buch* [buːx] "book," *Bücher* ['byːçɐ] "books"; *lachen* ['laxən] "laugh," *lächerlich* ['lɛçɐlɪç] "ridiculous."

2. At the beginning of a few words, *ch* is [ç], for example:

   Cherub ['çeːrʊp][3]   "cherub"

   China ['çiːna][3]   "China"

[k]

In a number of words of Greek origin, *ch* is pronounced [k]; learn to recognize the following:

1. Cha'rakter
2. Chor
3. Cho'ral
4. Christ
5. Melancho'lie[4]
6. Or'chester
7. Chronik
8. Chaos ['kaːɔs]
9. chaotisch [ka'oːtɪʃ]

---

[3] Also frequently pronounced with [k]: ['keːrʊp], ['kiːna]
[4] In Austria also with [ç]: [melaŋço'liː]

Exercise 15.1   Pronounce:

1. verachten, verächtlich, Buch, Bücher, durchaus
2. Loch, Löcher, hoch, höchste, Kirchhof
3. Flucht, flüchtig, Sprache, Gespräch, Fichte
4. flechten, flocht, sprechen, sprach, gesprochen
5. Gedächtnis, dachte, Geschichte, dicht, Psyche
6. miss'achten, Macht, mächtig, bezeichnet, Dolch
7. durchschleichen, melan'cholisch, Eiche, Caba'ret, Cä'cilie
8. Drache, christlich, Chor, Echo, Cy'presse
9. Rauch, räuchern, chi'nesisch, mochte, möchte

Excerpts   Read the following excerpts aloud:

1.

Ach! denkt das Veilchen, wär' ich nur	Oh, thinks the violet, (if) only I were
Die schönste Blume der Natur,	the loveliest flower in nature,
Ach! nur ein kleines Weilchen,	oh, just (for) a little while,
Bis mich das Liebchen abgepflückt	until my sweetheart picked me
Und an dem Busen matt gedrückt,	and crushed me to her bosom,
Ach nur, ach nur	oh just, oh just
Ein Viertelstündchen lang!	a quarter (of an) hour long!
Ach, aber ach! das Mädchen kam	Oh, but oh! the maiden came
Und nicht in acht das Veilchen nahm,	and took no note of the violet,
Ertrat das arme Veilchen...	trampled the poor violet...

Das Veilchen
Goethe/Mozart

2.

Ich möchte nicht mehr leben,	I want to live no longer,
Möcht' augenblicks verderben,	want instantly to perish,
Und möchte doch auch leben	und yet want also to live
Für dich, mit dir, und nimmer, nimmer sterben.	for you, with you, and never, never to die.
Ach, rede, sprich ein Wort nur,	Oh, speak, say one word only,
Ein einziges, ein klares ...	a single (word), a clear (one)…

Nicht mehr zu dir zu gehen
Daumer/Brahms

Recordings

Practice reading the text of the following song. Then record it without pausing.

Wehe, Lüftchen, lind und lieblich	Blow, little breeze, mild and soft,
Um die Wange der Geliebten,	about the cheek of my beloved,
Spiele zart in ihrer Locke,	play gently in her curls,
Eile nicht, hin'weg zu fliehn!	don't hurry to run away!
Tut sie dann vie'lleicht die Frage,	(If) she then perhaps asks the question
Wie es um mich Armen stehe;	how I, poor thing, am doing,
Sprich: "Un'endlich war sein Wehe,	say: "Unending was his pain,
Höchst bedenklich seine Lage;	most worrisome his condition;
Aber jetzo kann er hoffen,	But now he can hope
Wieder herrlich aufzuleben,	again fully to revive,
Denn du, Holde,	since you, fair (one),
Denkst an ihn."	are thinking of him!"

Botschaft
Daumer (after Hafis)/Brahms

Song   Sing the following song, paying special attention to the pronunciation of *ch*.

Freut euch des Lebens,	Find joy in living
Weil noch das Lämpchen glüht,	while yet the lamp's aglow,
Pflücket die Rose,	pick the rose
Eh' sie verblüht!	ere it fades!
Man schafft so gern sich Sorg' und Müh',	We make so gladly our own care and toil,
Sucht Dornen auf und findet sie	seek out thorns and find them
Und lässt das Veilchen unbemerkt,	and leave the violet unnoticed
Das uns am Wege blüht.	that along our way is blooming.
Freut euch des Lebens...	Find joy in living...
Wer Redlichkeit und Treue liebt	(If) one loves honesty and loyalty
Und gern dem ärmer'n Bruder gibt,	and gives gladly to the poorer brother,
Da siedelt sich Zufriedenheit	then contentment will come
So gerne bei ihm ein.	so readily to dwell within him.
Freut euch des Lebens...	Find joy in living...
Und wenn der Pfad sich furchtbar engt	And when (life's) path grows terribly narrow
Und Missgeschick sich plagt und drängt,	and misfortune plagues and presses,
Reicht die Freundschaft schwesterlich	friendship extends, like a sister,
Dem Redlichen die Hand.	to honest ones her hand.
Freut euch des Lebens...	Find joy in living...
Sie ist des Lebens schönstes Band,	It is life's loveliest bond,
Schlingt Brüder traulich Hand in Hand,	(and) links brothers harmoniously hand in hand,
So wallt man froh, so wallt man leicht	so we wander cheerfully, so we wander easily
Ins bess're Vaterland.	into a better land.
Freut euch des Lebens...	Find joy in living...

Freut euch des Lebens

Sorg' und Müh', sucht Dor - nen auf und fin - det sie und
Treu - e liebt und gern dem är - mern Bru - der gibt, da
furcht - bar engt und Miß - ge - schick sich plagt und drängt
schön - stes Band, schlingt Brü - der trau - lich Hand in Hand, so

D.C. al Fine

läßt das Veil - chen un - be - merkt, das uns am We - ge blüht.
sie - delt sich Zu - frie - den - heit so ger - ne bei ihm ein.
reicht die Freund-schaft schwes - ter - lich dem Red - li - chen die Hand.
wallt man froh, so wallt man leicht ins bess' - re Va - ter - land.

SECTION 3: *chs*

One Element [ks]

When *chs* occurs within one element, it is pronounced [ks], as in *wachsen* ['vaksən] "grow."

In the next section, on *chs* in two elements, we see a rather sizable number of forms in which *chs* is *not* pronounced [ks]; the singer should therefore become familiar with some common words containing *chs* within one element:

1.	Achse	"axle"	13.	Sachsen	"Saxony"
2.	Achsel	"shoulder"	14.	sechs	"six"
3.	Büchse	"rifle, box"	15.	Wachs	"wax"
4.	Dachs	"badger"	16.	wachsen	"grow"
5.	Deichsel	"shaft"		a. du wächst	"you grow"
6.	Drechsler	"turner"		b. er wächst	"he grows"
7.	Fuchs	"fox"		c. er wuchs	"he grew"
8.	Fuchsie ['fʊksiə]	"fuchsia"	17.	wechseln	"change"
9.	Gewächs	"growth"	18.	Weichsel	kind of cherry
10.	Lachs	"salmon"			
11.	Luchs	"lynx"			
12.	Ochse	"ox"			

Two Elements

When *ch* belongs to one element and s to the next, each must of course be pronounced with its element and in accordance with the rules for *ch* and *s* respectively.

1. *ch* + verb ending *-st:*

   du lachst [laxst] "you laugh" < *lachen*

   du weichst [vaɛçst] "you retreat" < *weichen*

2. *ch* + noun ending -*s*:
   des Bachs [baxs] "of the brook" <*Bach*
   des Blechs [blɛçs] "of the metal" < *Blech*

3. *ch* + superlative suffix -*st:*
   höchst [høːçst "highest"
   nächst- [nɛːçst] "nearest, next"
   herrlichsten ['hɛrlɪçstən] "most splendid"

4. Compounds:
   durchspielen ['dʊrçʃpiːlən] "play through"
   Lochsäge ['lɔx‚zɛːgə] "keyhole saw"

Exercise 15.2   Pronounce:

1. sechs, wechselt, wachsen, Fuchs, Buchs
2. erbleichst, Deichsel, Lachs, Bachs, lachst
3. sprichst, brichst, Gewächs, Gesprächs
4. Büchse, herrlichste, siegreichsten, Buchstabe
5. weichst, Weichsel, Königreichs, lieblichsten
6. huldreichstes, höchsten, nächste, wächst
7. Gebrauchs, Gefährlichsten, durchsetzen, wachsam

Exercise 15.3   Transcribe the words in Exercise 15.2 into the IPA.

16

The Sounds of *w, v, f*

SECTION 1: *w*
(LOWER-CASE W)

The letter *w* is almost always pronounced [v], as in *Wein* [vaẹn] "wine," *zwei* [tswaẹ] "two."

Exercise 16.1

Pronounce:

1. wo'her, gewohnt, entzwei, zwanzig, zwölf

2. schwarz, schwingen, wegwerfen, Löwe, wogten

3. Ju'wel, jeweils, Möwe, bewegt, beschwört

Excerpts

Read the following excerpts aloud:

1.

Jeder wird sich glücklich scheinen,	Everyone will think himself happy
Wenn mein Bild vor ihm erscheint,	when my face appears before him,
Eine Träne wird er weinen,	a tear will he weep,
Und ich weiß nicht, was er weint.	and I'll know not why he weeps.

Harfenspieler
Goethe/Wolf

2.

O wer sehen könnte, welche Bilder Hinter dieser Stirne, diesen schwarzen Wimpern sich in sanftem Wechsel malen!	Oh, could one see what images behind this brow, these dark lashes in gentle flow arise!

Schlafendes Jesuskind
Mörike/Wolf

 3.

Ach, es entschwindet mit tauigem Flügel Mir auf den wiegenden Wellen die Zeit. Morgen entschwinde mit schimmerndem Flügel Wieder wie gestern und heute die Zeit, Bis ich auf höherem strahlendem Flügel Selber entschwinde der wechselnden Zeit.	Alas, slipping away from me on dewy wing, on the rolling waves, is Time. Tomorrow may (it) vanish on shimmering wing again, like yesterday and today—Time, until I, upon a higher, radiant wing, myself vanish from this ever-changing Time.

Auf dem Wasser zu singen
Stolberg/Schubert

Song   Sing the following song, concentrating on the pronunciation of *w* (note that *v* is usually pronounced [f]).

Morgen will mein Schatz verreisen,	Tomorrow my sweetheart is going away,
Abschied nehmen mit Gewalt,	taking leave unwillingly,
Draußen singen schon die Vögel	outside the birds are already singing
In dem grünen, grünen Wald.	in the green, green forest.
Denn es fällt mir so schwer	Because it would be so hard for me
Aus der Heimat zu geh'n,	to go away from home,
Wenn die Hoffnung nicht wär'	if there weren't the hope
Auf ein Wiederseh'n,	of seeing each other again—
Lebe wohl, auf Wiederseh'n!	farewell, until we meet again!
Saßen da zwei Turteltauben,	There sat two turtle doves,
Saßen wohl auf grünem Ast.	sat upon a green branch.
Wo sich zwei Verliebte scheiden,	Where two lovers part,
Da verwelken Laub und Gras.	there leaves and grass will wither.
Denn es fällt mir so schwer...	Because it would be so hard...
Laub und Gras, das mag verwelken,	Leaves and grass, they may wither,
Aber uns're Liebe nicht.	but not our love.
Du kommst mir aus meinen Augen,	You'll be out of my sight,
Aber aus dem Herzen nicht.	but not out of my heart.
Denn es fällt mir so schwer...	Because it would be so hard...
Eine Schwalbe macht kein'n Sommer,	One swallow doesn't make a summer,
Ob sie gleich die erste ist;	even if it's the first;
Und mein Liebchen macht mir Kummer,	and my sweetheart causes me pain,
Ob sie gleich die Schönste ist.	even if she is the loveliest.
Denn es fällt mir so schwer, etc.	Because it would be so hard...

Morgen will mein Schatz verreisen

Hei - mat zu geh'n, wenn die Hoff - nung nicht wär' auf ein

Wie - der, Wie - der-sehn, le - be wohl, le - be wohl, le - be

wohl, le - be wohl, le - be wohl, auf Wie - der____ sehn!

SECTION 2: *v*

[f] (lower-case F)

In words of Germanic origin, *v* is pronounced [f], as in *viel* [fiːl] "much," *Bevölkerung* [bəˈfœlkərʊŋ] "population." It is pronounced [f] in:

Vers [fɛrs][1]	"verse"
Veilchen [ˈfaɛlçən]	"violet"
Vogt [foːkt]	"warden, governor"

[v] (lower-case V)

In most words of foreign origin, *v* is pronounced [v] before a vowel: *Vase* [ˈvaːzə], *Klavier* [klaˈviːɐ], *braver* [ˈbraːvɐ]. However, like *b*, *d*, *g*, and *s*, it becomes unvoiced in final position or before a consonant: *brav* [braːf], *bravster* [ˈbraːfstɐ].

Exercise 16.2

Pronounce:

1. Vater, völlig, vervollständigen, Vioˈline, vom
2. brave, brav, nerˈvös, Nerv, Villa, Venus
3. Klaˈvier, Frevel, Frevler, Proˈvinz, Noˈvember
4. Vetter, Noˈvelle, Viola, vieˈlleicht, Sklave
5. bevor, daˈvon, Virtuˈose, Veilchen, Vers, verweht
6. Levˈkoje, Tonverschiebung, Pulver, priˈvat, Universiˈtät

Exercise 16.3   Transcribe the above words into the IPA.

---

[1]The pronunciation [vɛrs] is also heard.

Excerpt   Read the following excerpt aloud.

So wandelt froh auf Gottes Wegen,	So wander joyously upon God's paths,
Und was ihr thut, das thut getreu!	and whatever you do, do it faithfully!
Verdienet eures Gottes Segen,	Earn your God's blessing,
Denn der ist alle Morgen neu:	for it is every morning new:
Denn welcher seine Zuversicht	for (if) one his trust
Auf Gott setzt, den verlässt er nicht.	in God will place, He will not abandon him.

Wer nur den lieben Gott lässt walten
Bach

SECTION 3: *f, ff*

f [f]

The letter *f* is always pronounced [f] as in *fein* [faęn] "fine," *Brief* [briːf] "letter," *gefragt* [gəˈfraːkt] "asked."

ff

One Element   When *ff* occurs within one element, it is pronounced [f], as in *treffen* [ˈtrɛfən] "meet," *trifft* [trɪft] "meets."

Two Elements   Occasionally, *ff* constitutes parts of two elements, in which case the *f* is extended, as in *auffahren* "rise," and the extended consonant may be represented with a tie bar: [ˈaǫf͡faːrən].

Exercise 16.4   Pronounce:

1. Fuge, fällen, führen, Efeu, rufen
2. Neffe, Ofen, offen, Öfen, öffnen
3. schlafe, schlaffe, aufliegen, auffliegen, auffallen
4. Stiefvater, aufragen, befragen, schroff, pfiff
5. Pfeife, Haufen, häufig, schafft, Schaft, verblüfft

Recording

Practice reading the lyrics of the following song. Then record them without pausing.

Wie Melodien zieht es
mir leise durch den Sinn,
wie Frühlingsblumen blüht es
und schwebt wie Duft dahin.

Doch kommt das Wort und fasst es
und führt es vor das Aug',
wie Nebelgrau erblasst es
und schwindet wie ein Hauch.

Und dennoch ruht im Reime
verborgen wohl ein Duft,
den mild aus stillem Keime
ein feuchtes Auge ruft.

Like melodies it drifts
softly through my mind,
like spring flowers it blooms
and wafts away like fragrance.

But (then) comes the word and grasps it
and brings it before my eyes;
like misty gray it fades
and vanishes like a breath.

And yet (there) remains in the rhyme
hidden still a fragrance
which, gently, from its stillness
a teary eye calls forth.

Wie Melodien zieht es mir
Groth/Brahms

17

The Sounds of *m*, *n*

SECTION 1: *m*, *mm*

m (lower-case M)

The letter *m* is pronounced [m], as in *mein* [maęn], "my," *kamen* [ˈkaːmən] "came."

mm

One Element

When it occurs in one element, *mm* is pronounced [m], as in *Flamme* [ˈflamə] "flame," *flammt* [flamt] "burns."[1]

Two Elements

When *mm* represents parts of two elements, as in *ummalen* "repaint," the pronunciation is extended, and the extended consonant may be represented with a tie bar: [ˈʊm͜maːlən].

---

[1]Some singers may extend the consonant, depending on expressive intention.

Excerpt   Read the following excerpt aloud:

Mach auf, mach auf, doch leise, mein Kind,	Open up, open up, but softly, my child,
Um keinen vom Schlummer zu wecken;	so that no one from slumber awakens;
Kaum murmelt der Bach, kaum zittert im Wind	scarcely murmurs the brook, scarcely trembles in the wind
Ein Blatt an den Büschen und Hecken.	any leaf on the bushes and hedges.
Drum leise, mein Mädchen, dass nichts sich regt,	So, softly, my girl, so that nothing stirs,
Nur leise die Hand auf die Klinke gelegt.	just softly place your hand on the door handle.

Ständchen
Schack/Strauß

SECTION 2: *n, nn, ng, nk*

n (lower-case N)

As in English, the letter *n* is pronounced as the voiced alveolar nasal [n]: *nein* [naɛn] "no," *blind* [blɪnt] "blind."

nn

One Element

When it occurs in one element, *nn* is pronounced [n], as in *Tanne* ['tanə] "fir," *nennt* [nɛnt] "calls."[2]

Two Elements

When *nn* represents parts of two elements, as in *annehmen* "assume," *hinnehmen* "accept," the pronunciation is extended, and the extended consonant may be represented with a tie bar: ['an͜neːmən], ['hɪn͜neːmən].

---

[2]Some singers may extend the consonant, depending on expressive intention.

ng

One Element   When *ng* occurs within one element it is always pronounced [ŋ], as in *Finger* ['fɪŋɐ] "finger," *Hunger* ['hʊŋɐ] "hunger," *Klang* [klaŋ] "sound."[3]

Two Elements   When *n* and *g* represent parts of two elements, they are pronounced as [n] + [g], as in *angehen* ['anˌgeːən] "concern," *hingehen* ['hɪnˌgeːən] "go there."

nk

One Element   When *nk* occurs within one element, it is always pronounced [ŋk], as in *dunkel* ['dʊŋkəl] "dark," *Dank* [daŋk] "thanks."

Two Elements   When *n* and *k* belong to different elements, they are pronounced as [n] + [k], as in *ankommen* ['anˌkɔmən] "arrive," *unklar* ['ʊnˌklaːɐ̯] "unclear."

Exercise 17.1   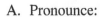 A. Pronounce:

1. Ring, Doppelgänger, Meistersinger, danken, denken

2. Hingabe, hing, hingehören, hinken, hinkommen

3. angelehnt, Engel, dringlich, grimmig, kommen

4. jüng'rem, Haingesträuch, Frühlingsabendrot, ˌrings'um

5. Engelszungen, Angebinde, Tränenahnung, hinnen, herannahen

6. Mondscheinnacht, kennen, ungeleitet, unnütz, Brunnen

7. Junggeselle, Gesangstunde, Gemeingut, Jammer

8. annehmen, dennoch, angenommen, Funktion, Spengler

9. Götterfunken, klangreich, klingen, Tonkunst, Junker-Unkraut

10. Drangsal, empfange, englisch, entlanggehen, Unglück

B. Transcribe the above words into the IPA.

---

[3]If *ng* is followed by a back vowel, it is pronounced [ŋg], e.g. *Ungarn* ['ʊŋgarn] "Hungary"; *Ungarisch* ['ʊŋgarɪʃ], "Hungarian." (Note that in a word like *ungar* "underdone," *un-* is a prefix; hence the pronunciation is ['ʊnˌgaːɐ̯].)

Exercise 17.2   Read the following transcription aloud:

[deːɐ̯ toːt, das |ɪst diː ˈkyːlə naxt,

das ˈleːbən |ɪst deːɐ̯ ˈʃvyːlə taːk.

|es ˈdʊŋkəlt ʃoːn, mɪç ˈʃleːfɐt,

deːɐ̯ taːk hat mɪç myːt gəˈmaxt.

ˈyːbɐ maɛ̯n bɛt |ɛɐ̯ˈheːpt zɪç |aɛ̯n baɔ̯m,

drɪn zɪŋt diː ˈjʊŋə ˈnaxtɪgal;

ziː zɪŋt fɔn ˈlaɔ̯tɐ ˈliːbə,

|ɪç høːɐ̯ |es zoˈgaːɐ̯ |ɪm traɔ̯m.]

Excerpts   Read the following excerpts aloud:

1.

Wie im Morgenglanze	How in the morning's splendor
Du rings mich anglühst,	you glow at me (from) all around,
Frühling, Geliebter!	Spring, beloved!

Ganymed
Goethe/Schubert

2.

Dein Angesicht, so lieb und schön,	Your countenance, so dear and lovely,
Das hab' ich jüngst im Traum geseh'n,	I saw it recently in a dream,
Es ist so mild und engelgleich,	it is so gentle and angelic,
Und doch so bleich, so schmerzenreich.	and yet so pale, so full of pain.

Dein Angesicht
Heine/Schumann

Recording

Practice reading the lyrics of the following song. Then record them without pausing.

Holder klingt der Vogelsang,
Wenn die Engelreine,
Die mein Jünglingsherz bezwang,
Wandelt durch die Haine.

Röter blühet Tal und Au,
Grüner wird der Rasen,
Wo die Finger meiner Frau
Maienblumen lasen.

Ohne sie ist alles tot,
Welk sind Blüt' und Kräuter;
Und kein Frühlingsabendrot
Dünkt mir schön und heiter.

Traute, minnigliche Frau
Wollest nimmer fliehen,
Dass mein Herz gleich dieser Au,
Mög' in Wonne blühen.

More lovely sounds the birdsong
when the purest angel
who conquered my young man's heart
strolls through the groves.

More brightly bloom valley and meadow,
greener grows the grass
where the fingers of my lady
picked May flowers.

Without her everything is dead,
wilted are blossoms and plants,
and no spring sunset
seems beautiful and cheerful to me.

Beloved, gracious lady,
may you never want to part,
so that my heart, like this meadow,
may bloom in delight.

Minnelied
Hölty/Brahms

Songs   Sing the following songs, concentrating on the sounds of *m* and *n*.

Ade zur guten Nacht,
Jetzt ist der Schluss gemacht,
Dass ich muss scheiden.
Im Sommer wächst der Klee,
Im Winter schneit's den Schnee:
Da komm' ich wieder.

Adieu as we say goodnight,
now the decision is made
that I must leave.
In the summer grows the clover,
in the winter snows the snow:
Then I'll come back.

Es trauern Berg und Tal,
Wo ich viel tausendmal
Bin drüber gangen.
Das hat deine Schönheit gemacht,
Hat mich zum Lieben gebracht
Mit großem Verlangen.

(There) Mountain and valley mourn
where I many thousands of times
have walked (over them).
Your beauty did it,
brought me to love
with great longing.

Das Brünnlein rinnt und rauscht
Wohl unterm Holderstrauch,
Da wir gesessen.
So manchen Glockenschlag,
Wo Herz bei Herzen lag,
Das hast vergessen.

The little spring flows and rushes
right under the elder bush
where we sat.
So many a church bell chiming,
where heart against heart lay,
(you) have forgotten that.

Die Mädchen in der Welt
Sind falscher als das Geld
Mit ihrem Lieben.
Ade zur guten Nacht,
Jetzt ist der Schluss gemacht,
Dass ich muss scheiden.

The girls of the world
are more false than money
with their loving.
Adieu as we say good night,
now the decision is made
that I must leave.

Ade, zur guten Nacht

A - de zur gu - ten Nacht, jetzt ist der Schluß ge - macht, daß
Es trau - ern Berg und Tal, wo ich viel tau - send - mal bin
Das Brünn - lein rinnt und rauscht wohl un - term Hol - der - strauch, da
Die Mäd - chen in der Welt sind fal - scher als das Geld mit

ich muß schei - den. Im Som - mer wächst der Klee, im
drü - ber gan - gen. Das hat dei - ne Schön - heit ge - macht, hat
wir ge - ses - sen. So man - chen Glok - ken - schlag, wo
ih - rem Lie - ben. A - de zur gu - ten Nacht, jetzt

Win - ter schneit's den Schnee: da komm' ich wie - der.
mich zum Lie - ben ge-bracht mit gro - ßem Ver - lan - gen.
Herz bei Her - zen lag, das hast ver - ges - sen.
ist der Schluß ge - macht, daß ich muß schei - den.

O Tannenbaum, o Tannenbaum,
wie treu sind deine Blätter!
Du grünst nicht nur zur Sommerszeit,
nein, auch im Winter, wenn es schneit.
O Tannenbaum, o Tannenbaum,
wie treu sind deine Blätter!

O Tannenbaum, o Tannenbaum,
du kannst mir sehr gefallen.
Wie oft hat nicht zur Weihnachtszeit
ein Baum von dir mich hoch erfreut.
O Tannenbaum...

O Tannenbaum, o Tannenbaum,
dein Kleid will mich was lehren.
Die Hoffnung und Beständigkeit
gibt Trost und Kraft zu jeder Zeit.
O Tannenbaum...

O fir tree, o fir tree,
how faithful are your leaves!
You're green not only in summertime,
no, also in winter, when it snows.
O fir tree, or fir tree,
how faithful are your leaves!

O fir tree, o fir tree,
you (can) please me greatly.
How often has (not) at Christmastime
(the sight) of you delighted me.
O fir tree...

O fir tree, o fir tree,
your garment will teach me something.
Hope and constancy
give comfort and strength at all times.
O fir tree...

O Tannenbaum

O Tan - nen - baum, o Tan - nen - baum, wie treu sind dei - ne
O Tan - nen - baum, o Tan - nen - baum, du kannst mir sehr ge -
O Tan - nen - baum, o Tan - nen - baum, dein Kleid will mich was

Blät - ter! Du grünst nicht nur zur Som - mers - zeit nein
fal - len. Wie oft hat nicht zur Weih - nachts - zeit ein
leh - ren. Die Hoff - nung und Be - stän - dig - keit gibt

auch im Win - ter, wenn es schneit. O Tan - nen - baum, o
Baum von dir mich hoch er - freut. O Tan - nen - baum, o
Trost und Kraft zu je - der Zeit. O Tan - nen - baum, o

Tan - nen - baum, wie treu sind dei - ne Blät - ter!
Tan - nen - baum, du kannst mir sehr ge - fal - len.
Tan - nen - baum, dein Kleid will mich was leh - ren.

APPENDIX A

Charts

CHART 1. English Consonants

		Bilabial	Labiodental	Dental	Alveolar	Postalveolar	Palatal	Velar	Glottal
Stop	voiced	[b]			[d]			[g]	
	voiceless	[p]			[t]			[k]	
Fricative	voiced		[v]	[ð]	[z]	[ʒ]			
	voiceless		[f]	[θ]	[s]	[ʃ]			[h]
Affricate	voiced					[dʒ]			
	voiceless					[tʃ]			
Nasal	voiced	[m]			[n]			[ŋ]	
Lateral	voiced				[l]				
Trill	voiced				[ɾ]				
Approximant	voiced				[ɹ]				
Glide	voiced	[w]					[j]		

CHART 2. German Consonants

		Bilabial	Labiodental	Dental	Alveolar	Postalveolar	Palatal	Velar	Uvular	Glottal
Stop	voiced	[b]			[d]			[g]		
	voiceless	[p]			[t]			[k]		[ʔ]
Fricative	voiced		[v]		[z]	[ʒ]				
	voiceless		[f]		[s]	[ʃ]	[ç]	[x]	[χ]	[h]
Affricate	voiced									
	voiceless		[pf]		[ts]	[tʃ]				
Nasal	voiced	[m]			[n]			[ŋ]		
Lateral	voiced				[l]					
Trill	voiced				[r]					
Glide	voiced						[j]			

CHART 3. English Vowels

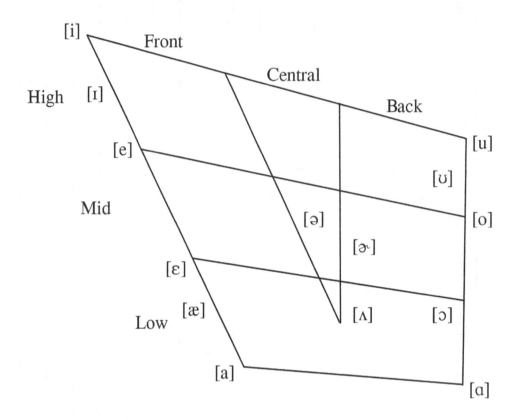

CHART 4. German Vowels

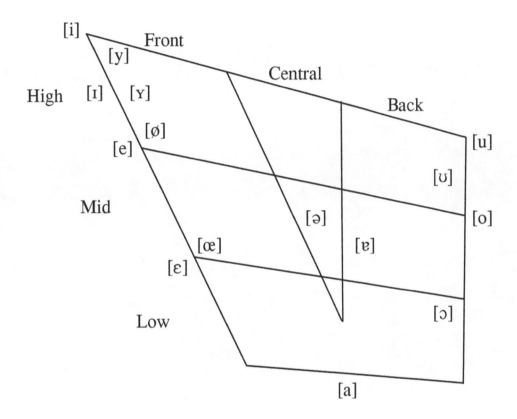

APPENDIX B

Additional Song Texts

Brahms: *Vergebliches Ständchen* (Futile Serenade)

Guten Abend, mein Schatz,	Good evening, my treasure,
Guten Abend, mein Kind!	good evening, my child!
Ich komm' aus Lieb' zu dir,	I come out of love to you,
Ach, mach' mir auf die Tür!	oh, open up the door for me!
Mach' mir auf die Tür!	Open up the door for me!
"Mein' Tür ist verschlossen,	"My door is locked,
Ich lass' dich nicht ein;	I'll not let you in;
Mutter, die rät mir klug,	Mother, she advises me wisely,
Wärst du herein mit Fug,	were you (to come) in here with permission,
Wär's mit mir vorbei!"	it would be all over for me!"
So kalt ist die Nacht,	So cold is the night,
So eisig der Wind,	so icy the wind,
Dass mir das Herz erfriert,	that my heart will freeze,
Mein' Lieb' erlöschen wird;	my love will be extinguished;
Öffne mir, mein Kind!	open up for me, my child!
"Löschet dein' Lieb',	"(If) your love is extinguished,
Lass sie löschen nur!	let it go out, then!
Löschet sie immer zu,	(Even if) it goes out forever,
Geh' heim zu Bett, zur Ruh',	go home to bed, to rest!
Gute Nacht, mein Knab'!"	Good night, my boy!"

FOLK SONG

Schubert: *An die Musik* (To Music)

Du holde Kunst, in wieviel grauen Stunden,	You lovely art, in how many gray hours,
Wo mich des Lebens wilder Kreis umstrickt,	when life's wild circle ensnared me,
Hast du mein Herz zu warmer Lieb' entzunden,	have you ignited my heart to warm love,
Hast mich in eine bess're Welt entrückt!	(and) transported me into a better world!
Oft hat ein Seufzer, deiner Harf' entflossen,	Often has a sigh, from your harp flowing,
Ein süßer, heiliger Akkord von dir,	a sweet, holy chord of yours,
Den Himmel bess'rer Zeiten mir erschlossen,	the Heaven of better times revealed to me,
Du holde Kunst, ich danke dir dafür!	you lovely art, I thank you for that!

SCHOBER

Schubert: *Du bist die Ruh'* (You Are Peace)

Du bist die Ruh',	You are peace,
Der Friede mild,	gentle peace,
Die Sehnsucht du,	longing, you,
Und was sie stillt.	and what calms it.
Ich weihe dir	I dedicate to you,
Voll Lust und Schmerz	full of desire and pain,
Zur Wohnung hier	as a dwelling here,
Mein Aug' und Herz.	my eye and heart.
Kehr ein bei mir	Come inside
Und schließe du	and close
Still hinter dir	quietly behind you
Die Pforten zu!	the gates!
Treib andern Schmerz	Drive other pain
Aus dieser Brust!	from this breast!
Voll sei dies Herz	Full be this heart
Von deiner Lust.	of your delight!
Dies Augenzelt	(My) world
Von deinem Glanz	by your splendor
Allein erhellt,	alone illuminated,
O füll es ganz!	oh, fill it completely!

RÜCKERT

Schubert: *Erlkönig* (Erlking)

Wer reitet so spät durch Nacht und Wind?
Es ist der Vater mit seinem Kind;
Er hat den Knaben wohl in dem Arm,
Er faßt ihn sicher, er hält ihn warm.

Mein Sohn, was birgst du so bang dein Gesicht?
Siehst, Vater, du den Erlkönig nicht?
Den Erlenkönig mit Kron' und Schweif?
Mein Sohn, es ist ein Nebelstreif.

"Du liebes Kind, komm, geh mit mir!
Gar schöne Spiele spiel' ich mit dir,
Manch bunte Blumen sind an dem Strand,
Meine Mutter hat manch gülden Gewand."

Mein Vater, mein Vater, und hörest du nicht,
Was Erlenkönig mir leise verspricht?
Sei ruhig, bleibe ruhig, mein Kind:
In dürren Blättern säuselt der Wind.

"Willst, feiner Knabe, du mit mir gehn?
Meine Töchter sollen dich warten schön;
Meine Töchter führen den nächtlichen Reihn
Und wiegen und tanzen und singen dich ein."

Mein Vater, mein Vater, und siehst du nicht dort
Erlkönigs Töchter am düstern Ort?
Mein Sohn, mein Sohn, ich seh' es genau:
Es scheinen die alten Weiden so grau.

"Ich liebe dich, mich reizt deine schöne Gestalt;
Und bist du nicht willig, so brauch' ich Gewalt."
Mein Vater, mein Vater, jetzt faßt er mich an!
Erlkönig hat mir ein Leids getan!

Dem Vater grauset's, er reitet geschwind,
Er hält in Armen das ächzende Kind,
Erreicht den Hof mit Mühe und Not;
In seinen Armen das Kind war tot.

Who rides so late through night and wind?
It is the father with his child;
he has the boy secure in his arm,
he holds him tightly, he keeps him warm.

My son, why do you hide so anxiously your face?
Do you, Father, not see the Erlking?
The Erlking with crown and train?
My son, it is a strip of mist.

"You dear child, come, go with me!
Quite lovely games I'll play with you.
Many colorful flowers are along the shore,
my mother has many a golden garment."

My father, my father, and do you not hear
what Erlking quietly promises me?
Be calm, stay calm, my child:
in dry leaves rustles the wind.

"Will, fine boy, you go with me?
My daughters shall wait on you nicely;
My daughters lead the nightly (round) dance
and (will) rock and dance and sing you to sleep."

My father, my father, and don't you see there
Erlking's daughters in that dark place?
My son, my son, I see it exactly:
There shine the old willows so gray.

"I love you, your beautiful form delights me;
and (if) you are not willing, then I'll use force."
My father, my father, now he takes hold of me!
Erlking has done me harm!

The father feels dread, he rides swiftly,
he holds in (his) arms the moaning child,
reaches the farmyard with effort and distress;
in his arms the child was dead.

GOETHE

Schubert: *Die Forelle* (The Trout)

In einem Bächlein helle,	In a little brook clear
Da schoss in froher Eil'	there shot in cheerful haste
Die launische Forelle	the capricious trout
Vorüber wie ein Pfeil.	past like an arrow.
Ich stand an dem Gestade,	I stood on the bank
Und sah in süßer Ruh'	and watched in sweet repose
Des muntern Fischleins Bade	the merry little fish swimming
Im klaren Bächlein zu.	in the clear brook.
Ein Fischer mit der Rute	A fisherman with his rod
Wohl an dem Ufer stand,	right on the shore was standing,
Und sah's mit kaltem Blute,	and watched with cold blood
Wie sich das Fischlein wand.	as the little fish twisted (itself).
So lang dem Wasser helle,	As long as the clear water,
So dacht' ich, nicht gebricht,	so thought I, (is) not disturbed,
So fängt er die Forelle	then he'll not catch the trout
Mit seiner Angel nicht.	with his rod.
Doch plötzlich ward dem Diebe	But suddenly for the thief
Die Zeit zu lang. Er macht	the time became too long. He makes
Das Bächlein tückisch trübe,	the little brook treacherously cloudy,
Und eh' ich es gedacht,	and before I could think,
So zuckte seine Rute,	his pole twitched,
Das Fischlein zappelt dran,	(and) the little fish is wriggling on it,
Und ich mit regem Blute	and I with blood aboil
Sah die Betrogne an.	looked at the deceived (one).

SCHUBART

Schubert: *Gretchen am Spinnrade* (Gretchen at the Spinning Wheel)

Meine Ruh ist hin,	My peace is gone,
Mein Herz ist schwer;	my heart is heavy;
Ich finde sie nimmer	I will find it never,
Und nimmermehr.	(and) never again.
Wo ich ihn nicht hab'	Wherever I don't have him
Ist mir das Grab,	is for me the grave,
Die ganze Welt	the whole world
Ist mir vergällt.	has become bitter for me.

Mein armer Kopf	My poor head
Ist mir verrückt,	(seems) crazed to me,
Mein armer Sinn	my poor mind
Ist mir zerstückt.	has gone to pieces.
Meine Ruh ist hin,	My peace is gone,
Mein Herz ist schwer;	my heart is heavy;
Ich finde sie nimmer	I will find it never,
Und nimmermehr.	(and) never again.
Nach ihm nur schau' ich	For him only I look
Zum Fenster hinaus,	out the window,
Nach ihm nur geh' ich	for him only I go
Aus dem Haus.	out of the house.
Sein hoher Gang,	His proud gait,
Sein' edle Gestalt,	his noble form,
Seines Mundes Lächeln,	(the) smile of his mouth,
Seiner Augen Gewalt,	(the) power of his eyes,
Und seiner Rede	and his speech,
Zauberfluß,	(the) magic flow,
Sein Händedruck,	the touch of his hand,
Und ach, sein Kuß!	and, oh, his kiss!
Meine Ruh ist hin,	My peace is gone,
Mein Herz ist schwer;	my heart is heavy;
Ich finde sie nimmer	I will find it never,
Und nimmermehr.	(and) never again.
Mein Busen drängt	My bosom urges
Sich nach ihm hin;	(me) to him;
Ach, dürft' ich fassen	oh, (if only) I might touch
Und halten ihn	and hold him
Und küssen ihn,	and kiss him
So wie ich wollt',	as I wished,
An seinen Küssen	amid his kisses
Vergehen sollt'!	I should perish!

GOETHE

Schubert: *Die junge Nonne* (The Young Nun)

Wie braust durch die Wipfel der heulende Sturm!	How roars through the treetops the howling storm!
Es klirren die Balken, es zittert das Haus!	the beams shaking, the house trembling,
Es rollet der Donner, es leuchtet der Blitz,	the thunder rolling, the lightning flashing,
Und finster die Nacht wie das Grab!	and dark (is) the night like the grave!
Immerhin, immerhin,	Indeed, indeed,
So tobt' es auch jüngst noch in mir!	there (was) also such raging just recently in me!
Es brauste das Leben, wie jetzo der Sturm,	Life roared as just now the storm,
Es bebten die Glieder, wie jetzo das Haus,	my limbs shook as just now the house,
Es flammte die Liebe, wie jetzo der Blitz,	love flared as just now the lightning,
Und finster die Brust wie das Grab!	and dark (was) my heart like the grave!
Nun tobe, du wilder, gewalt'ger Sturm,	Now rage, you wild, violent storm,
Im Herzen ist Friede, im Herzen ist Ruh',	in my heart is peace, in my heart is calm,
Des Bräutigams harret die liebende Braut,	the loving bride awaits her bridegroom,
Gereinigt in prüfender Glut,	purified in a trial of fire,
Der ewigen Liebe getraut.	to eternal love betrothed.
Ich harre, mein Heiland, mit sehnendem Blick!	I wait, my Savior, with longing gaze!
Komm, himmlischer Bräutigam, hole die Braut,	Come, heavenly bridegroom, fetch your bride,
Erlöse die Seele von irdischer Haft!	Release this soul from earthly confinement!
Horch, friedlich ertönet das Glöcklein vom Turm!	Hark, peacefully peals the little bell from the tower!
Es lockt mich das süße Getön	It calls me, the sweet ringing,
Allmächtig zu ewigen Höh'n.	all-powerfully to eternal heights.
Alleluja!	Alleluja!

CRAIGHER

Schubert: *Der Tod und das Mädchen* (Death and the Maiden)

DAS MÄDCHEN	The Maiden
Vorüber, ach vorüber!	(Go) past, oh, (go) past!
Geh, wilder Knochenmann!	Go, wild bone-man!
Ich bin noch jung! Geh, Lieber,	I am still young! Go, dear one,
Und rühre mich nicht an!	and touch me not!
DER TOD	Death
Gib deine Hand, du schön und zart Gebild!	Give (me) your hand, you lovely and delicate vision!
Bin Freund und komme nicht zu strafen.	(I) am (a) friend and come not to punish.
Sei gutes Muts! Ich bin nicht wild,	Be of good cheer! I am not wild,
Sollst sanft in meinen Armen schlafen!	(you) shall sleep gently in my arms!

CLAUDIUS

Schubert: *Wohin?* (Whither?)

Ich hört' ein Bächlein rauschen	I heard a little brook rushing
Wohl aus dem Felsenquell,	out of its rocky source,
Hinab zum Tale rauschen	downward to the valley rushing,
So frisch und wunderhell.	so fresh and wonderfully clear.
Ich weiß nicht, wie mir wurde,	I know not what came over me,
Nicht, wer den Rat mir gab,	nor who gave me the advice,
Ich musste auch hinunter	I too had to (go) down there
Mit meinem Wanderstab.	with my walking stick.
Hinunter und immer weiter,	Downward and ever further,
Und immer dem Bache nach,	and always along the brook;
Und immer frischer rauschte,	and ever more briskly was rushing,
Und immer heller der Bach.	and ever more brightly, the brook.
Ist das denn meine Straße?	Is this then my path?
O Bächlein, sprich, wohin?	Oh, little brook, speak, where to?
Du hast mit deinem Rauschen	You have with your rushing
Mir ganz berauscht den Sinn.	wholly enchanted my mind.
Was sag' ich denn vom Rauschen?	Why then do I say rushing?
Das kann kein Rauschen sein!	This cannot be rushing!
Es singen wohl die Nixen	It is surely the water nymphs singing,
Tief unten ihren Reihn.	deep below, their songs.
Lass singen, Gesell, lass rauschen,	Let (there be) singing, comrade, let (there be) rushing,
Und wandre fröhlich nach!	and wander cheerfully after (it)!
Es gehn ja Mühlenräder	(For) indeed millwheels turn
In jedem klaren Bach.	in every clear brook!

MÜLLER

Schumann: *Du bist wie eine Blume* (You Are Like a Flower)

Du bist wie eine Blume
So hold und schön und rein;
Ich schau' dich an, und Wehmut
Schleicht mir ins Herz hinein.

Mir ist, als ob ich die Hände
Aufs Haupt dir legen sollt'
Betend, daß Gott dich erhalte
So rein und schön und hold.

You are like a flower,
so fair and lovely and pure;
I look at you, and melancholy
creeps into my heart.

(I feel) as if I my hands
upon your head should lay,
praying that God keep you
so pure and lovely and fair.

HEINE

Schumann: *Du Ring an meinem Finger* (You Ring on my Finger)

Du Ring an meinem Finger,
Mein goldenes Ringelein,
Ich drücke dich fromm an die Lippen,
Dich fromm an das Herze mein.

Ich hatt' ihn ausgeträumet,
Der Kindheit friedlich schönen Traum,
Ich fand allein mich, verloren
Im öden, unendlichen Raum.

Du Ring an meinem Finger,
Da hast du mich erst belehrt,
Hast meinem Blick erschlossen
Des Lebens unendlichen Wert.

Ich werd' ihm dienen, ihm leben,
Ihm angehören ganz,
Hin selber mich geben und finden
Verklärt mich in seinem Glanz.

Du Ring an meinem Finger,
Mein goldenes Ringelein,
Ich drücke dich fromm an die Lippen,
Dich fromm an das Herze mein.

You ring on my finger,
My golden little ring,
I press you devoutly to my lips,
(you) devoutly to this heart (of) mine.

I had finished dreaming it,
childhood's peacefully lovely dream,
I found myself alone, lost
in a desolate, endless space.

You ring on my finger,
you first taught me,
(and) to my eyes revealed
life's infinite value.

I will serve him, live for him,
to him belong entirely,
(to him) give myself and find
myself transfigured in his splendor.

You ring on my finger,
my golden little ring,
I press you devoutly to my lips,
(you) devoutly to this heart (of) mine.

CHAMISSO

Schumann: *Frühlingsnacht* (Spring Night)

Über'm Garten durch die Lüfte
Hört' ich Wandervögel ziehn,
Das bedeutet Frühlingsdüfte,
Unten fängt's schon an zu blühn.

Jauchzen möcht' ich, möchte weinen,
Ist mir's doch, als könnt's nicht sein,
Alte Wunder wieder scheinen
Mit dem Mondesglanz herein.

Und der Mond, die Sterne sagen's,
Und im Traume rauscht's der Hain,
Und die Nachtigallen schlagen's:
Sie ist deine, sie ist dein!

Above the garden through the breezes
I heard birds flying past.
That heralds spring fragrances,
(here) below it's already beginning to bloom.

I'd like to shout, would like to weep,
I feel, though, as (if) it could not be—
old wonders again are beaming,
with the moon's glow, this way.

And the moon, the stars, are saying it,
and in a dream the grove is rustling it,
and the nightingales are singing it:
she is yours, she is yours!

EICHENDORFF

Schumann: *Ich grolle nicht* (I'll Not Be Bitter)

Ich grolle nicht, und wenn das Herz auch bricht,
Ewig verlor'nes Lieb! Ich grolle nicht.
Wie du auch strahlst in Diamantenpracht,
Es fällt kein Strahl in deines Herzens Nacht.

Das weiß ich längst. Ich sah dich ja im Traume,
Und sah die Nacht in deines Herzens Raume,
Und sah die Schlang', die dir am Herzen frisst,
Ich sah, mein Lieb, wie sehr du elend bist.
Ich grolle nicht.

I'll not be bitter, and even if my heart is breaking,
eternally lost love! I'll not be bitter.
Though you (may) shine in diamond-splendor,
there falls no ray (of light) into your heart's night.

This I've long known. I saw you (once) in a dream,
and saw the night within your heart's emptiness,
and saw the serpent that eats at your heart;
I saw, my love, how very pitiful you are.
I'll not be bitter.

HEINE

Schumann: *Die Lotosblume* (The Lotus Flower)

Die Lotosblume ängstigt	The lotus flower distresses
Sich vor der Sonne Pracht,	herself at the sun's splendor,
Und mit gesenktem Haupte	and with bowed head
Erwartet sie träumend die Nacht.	she awaits, dreaming, the night.
Der Mond, der ist ihr Buhle,	The moon, he is her lover,
Er weckt sie mit seinem Licht,	he awakens her with his light,
Und ihm entschleiert sie freundlich	and for him she unveils sweetly
Ihr frommes Blumengesicht	her innocent flower-face.
Sie blüht und glüht und leuchtet	She blooms and glows and beams
Und starret stumm in die Höh';	and gazes mutely into the sky;
Sie duftet und weinet und zittert	she is fragrant and weeping and trembling
Vor Liebe und Liebesweh.	with love and love's pain.

HEINE

Schumann: *Mondnacht* (Moon[lit] Night)

Es war, als hätt' der Himmel	It was as if Heaven had
Die Erde still geküsst,	quietly kissed the earth,
Dass sie im Blütenschimmer	(so) that she (earth), in a blossom-shimmer,
Von ihm nur träumen müsst'.	of him (Heaven) only had to dream.
Die Luft ging durch die Felder,	The breeze blew through the fields,
Die Ähren wogten sacht,	the grain swayed gently,
Es rauschten leis die Wälder,	the woods softly rustled,
So sternklar war die Nacht.	so starry-clear was the night.
Und meine Seele spannte	And my soul spread
Weit ihre Flügel aus,	out wide its wings,
Flog durch die stillen Lande,	flew through the silent lands,
Als flöge sie nach Haus.	as (if) it were flying home.

EICHENDORFF

Strauss: *Traum durch die Dämmerung* (Dream Through the Twilight)

Weite Wiesen im Dämmergrau;
Die Sonne verglomm, die Sterne ziehn;
Nun geh' ich hin zu der schönsten Frau,
Weit über Wiesen im Dämmergrau,
Tief in den Busch von Jas'min.

Durch Dämmergrau in der Liebe Land;
Ich gehe nicht schnell, ich eile nicht;
Mich zieht ein weiches, samtenes Band
Durch Dämmergrau in der Liebe Land,
In ein mildes, blaues Licht.

Broad meadows in the twilight-gray;
the sun (has) faded, the stars appear;
now I'll go to the loveliest woman,
far over meadows in the twilight-gray,
deep into the bushes of jasmine.

Through twilight-gray into love's land;
I go not quickly, I hurry not;
pulling me (is) a soft, velvet ribbon
through twilight-gray into love's land,
into a gentle blue light.

BIERBAUM

Strauss: *Morgen* (Tomorrow)

Und morgen wird die Sonne wieder scheinen,
Und auf dem Wege, den ich gehen werde,
Wird uns, die Glücklichen, sie wieder einen,
Inmitten dieser sonnenatmenden Erde…

Und zu dem Strand, dem weiten, wogenblauen,
Werden wir still und langsam niedersteigen.
Stumm werden wir uns in die Augen schauen,
Und auf uns sinkt des Glückes stummes Schweigen.

And tomorrow the sun will shine again,
and on the path which I shall take
(it) will again unite us, the happy ones,
in the midst of this sun-breathing earth…

and to the shore, (so) broad, wave-blue,
we shall quietly and slowly descend.
Mutely we shall look into each other's eyes,
(as) upon us settles the mute silence of happiness.

MACKAY

Wolf: *A'nakreons Grab* (Anacreon's Grave)

Wo die Rose hier blüht, wo Reben um Lorbeer sich
    schlingen,
Wo das Turtelchen lockt, wo sich das Grillchen ergötzt,
Welch ein Grab ist hier, das alle Götter mit Leben
Schön bepflanzt und geziert? Es ist A'nakreons Ruh'.

Frühling, Sommer und Herbst genoß der glückliche
    Dichter;
Vor dem Winter hat ihn endlich der Hügel geschützt.

Where the rose here blooms, where grapevines round
    laurel themselves entwine,
where the turtledove coos, where the cricket rejoices,
what grave is this that all gods with life
(so) beautifully (have) planted and adorned? It is
Anakreon's resting place.

Spring, Summer and Autumn gladdened the happy
    poet;
from the Winter, at the end, this mound has protected
    him

GOETHE

Wolf: *Er ist's* (It's Here)

Frühling lässt sein blaues Band	Spring sends its blue ribbon
Wieder flattern durch die Lüfte;	again fluttering through the breezes;
Süße, wohlbekannte Düfte	sweet, well-known fragrances
Streifen ahnungsvoll das Land.	brush, full of portent, (against) the earth.
Veilchen träumen schon,	Violets are dreaming already,
Wollen balde kommen.	(and) will soon appear.
Horch, von fern ein leiser Harfenton!	Hark, from afar a soft harp tone!
Frühling, ja du bist's!	Spring, yes, it's you!
Dich hab' ich vernommen!	(It's) you I've sensed!

MÖRIKE

Wolf: *Mignon-1*

Kennst du das Land, wo die Zi'tronen blühn,	Do you know the land where the lemons bloom,
Im dunkeln Laub die Gold-O'rangen glühn,	in the dark foliage the golden oranges glow,
Ein sanfter Wind vom blauen Himmel weht,	a gentle wind from the blue sky wafts,
Die Myrte still und hoch der Lorbeer steht?	the myrtle silent, and lofty the laurel stands?
Kennst du es wohl?	Do you know it perhaps?
Dahin! Dahin!	There! There!
Möcht' ich mit dir, o mein Geliebter, ziehn.	I long with you, oh, my beloved, to go.
Kennst du das Haus? Auf Säulen ruht sein Dach,	Do you know the house? Upon columns rests its roof,
Es glänzt der Saal, es schimmert das Gemach,	the great hall gleams, the chamber shimmmers,
Und Marmorbilder stehn und sehn mich an:	and marble statues stand and look at me:
Was hat man dir, du armes Kind, getan?	What have they done to you, you poor child?
Kennst du es wohl?	Do you know it perhaps?
Dahin! Dahin!	There! There!
Möcht' ich mit dir, o mein Beschützer, ziehn.	I long with you, oh, my protector, to go.
Kennst du den Berg und seinen Wolkensteg?	Do you know the mountain and its cloud-cloaked path?
Das Maultier sucht im Nebel seinen Weg;	The mule seeks in the mist its way;
In Höhlen wohnt der Drachen alte Brut;	in caves lives the old brood of dragons;
Es stürzt der Fels und über ihn die Flut.	the cliff falls (steeply) and over it the torrent.
Kennst du ihn wohl?	Do you know it perhaps?
Dahin! Dahin	There! There!
Geht unser Weg; o Vater, lass uns ziehn!	leads our path; oh, Father, let us go!

GOETHE

Wolf: *Mignon-3*

Nur wer die Sehnsucht kennt,	Only (one) who knows longing
Weiß, was ich leide!	knows what I suffer!
Allein und abgetrennt	Alone and cut off
Von aller Freude	from all joy
Seh' ich ans Firma'ment	I gaze into the heavens
Nach jener Seite.	in that direction.
Ach! der mich liebt und kennt,	Ah, he who loves and knows me
Ist in der Weite.	is far away.
Es schwindelt mir, es brennt	I feel dizzy, there's burning
Mein Eingeweide.	inside me.
Nur wer die Sehnsucht kennt	Only (one) who knows longing
Weiß was ich leide!	knows what I suffer!

GOETHE

Wolf: *Verborgenheit* (Seclusion)

Lass, o Welt, o lass mich sein!	Let, oh world, oh let me be!
Locket nicht mit Liebesgaben,	Tempt not with love's gifts,
Lasst dies Herz alleine haben	let this heart (in seclusion) have
Seine Wonne, seine Pein!	its ecstasy, its pain!
Was ich traure, weiß ich nicht,	Whatever I mourn, I know not,
Es ist unbekanntes Wehe;	it is unknown pain;
Immerdar durch Tränen sehe	always through tears I see
Ich der Sonne liebes Licht.	the sun's dear light.
Oft bin ich mir kaum bewusst,	Often I am barely aware (of) myself,
Und die helle Freude zücket	and bright joy flashes,
Durch die Schwere, so mich drücket,	through the weight so oppressing me,
Wonniglich in meiner Brust.	ecstatically in my breast.
Lass, o Welt, o lass mich sein!	Let, oh world, oh let me be!
Locket nicht mit Liebesgaben,	Tempt not with love's gifts,
Lasst dies Herz alleine haben	let this heart (in seclusion) have
Seine Wonne, seine Pein!	its ecstasy, its pain.

MÖRIKE

Wolf: *Das verlassene Mägdlein* (The Abandoned Maid)

Früh, wann die Hähne krähn,	Early, when the cocks crow,
Eh' die Sternlein schwinden,	before the little stars disappear,
Muss ich am Herde stehn,	I must stand at the hearth,
Muss Feuer zünden.	must light (the) fire.
Schön ist der Flammen Schein,	Lovely is the glow of the flames,
Es springen die Funken;	the sparks are leaping;
Ich schaue so drein,	I just stare at them,
In Leid versunken.	sunk in pain.
Plötzlich, da kommt es mir,	Suddenly, it comes to me,
Treuloser Knabe,	faithless boy,
Dass ich die Nacht von dir	that I last night of you
Geträumet habe.	did dream.
Träne auf Träne dann	Tear upon tear then
Stürzet hernieder;	flows down;
So kommt der Tag heran—	so arrives the day—
O ging' er wieder!	oh, would it leave again!

MÖRIKE

Schubert: *Die Post*

Von der Straβe her ein Posthorn klingt. Was hat es, dass es so hoch aufspringt, Mein Herz?	From the road a posthorn sounds. What is it, that it leaps so high, my heart?
Die Post bringt keinen Brief für dich. Was drängst du denn so wunderlich, Mein Herz?	The post brings no letter for you. Why then do you pound so strangely, my heart?
Nun ja, die Post kommt aus der Stadt, Wo ich ein liebes Liebchen hatt', Mein Herz!	Well yes, the post comes from the town where I had a dear sweetheart, my heart!
Willst wohl einmal hinüberseh'n, Und fragen, wie es dort mag geh'n, Mein Herz?	(Do you) want to take a look and ask how things may be going (over) there, my heart?

MÜLLER

Schubert, Die Post

Von der Straße her ein Posthorn klingt.
Was hat es, daß es so hoch aufspringt,
Mein Herz?

From the road a posthorn sounds.
What is it that makes you leap so high,
my heart?

Die Post bringt keinen Brief für dich.
Was drängst du denn so wunderlich,
Mein Herz?

The post brings no letter for you.
Why do you surge so strangely,
my heart?

Nun ja, die Post kommt aus der Stadt,
Wo ich ein liebes Liebchen hatt',
Mein Herz!

Well yes, the post comes from the town
where I once had a dear sweetheart,
my heart!

Willst wohl einmal hinüberseh'n
Und fragen, wie es dort mag geh'n,
Mein Herz?

Then you'll want to look over there
and ask, how things are going there,
my heart!

MÜLLER